THERE GOES THE NEIGHBOURHOOD

MICHAEL WESLEY is the executive director of the Lowy Institute for International Policy. Previously he was Professor of International Relations and director of the Griffith Asia Institute at Griffith University. Prior to this, he was the assistant director-general for Transnational Issues at the Office of National Assessments, and a senior lecturer in International Relations at the University of New South Wales. Between 2007 and 2009, Dr Wesley was the editor of the *Australian Journal of International Affairs*. He has served on the Australian Research Council's College of Experts and the Queensland Art Gallery's Board of Trustees. He is a visiting professor at Griffith University and the University of Sydney, and a non-resident fellow of the Brookings Institution.

THERE GOES THE NEIGHBOURHOOD

Australia and the Rise of Asia

Michael Wesley

NEW
SOUTH

A New South book

Published by
University of New South Wales Press Ltd
University of New South Wales
Sydney NSW 2052
AUSTRALIA
www.unswpress.com.au

National Library of Australia Cataloguing-in-Publication entry
    Author: Wesley, Michael, 1968–
    Title: There goes the neighbourhood: Australia and the rise of Asia/by
    Michael Wesley.
    ISBN: 978 174223 272 0 (pbk.)
    Series: Lowy Institute series; Book 1
    Subjects: Australia – Relations – Asia.
        Asia – Relations – Australia.
    Dewey Number: 303.4829405

Design Avril Makula
Cover Nada Backovic Design
Front cover image iStockphoto
Author photo Peter Morris
Printer Ligare

This book is printed on paper using fibre supplied from plantation or sustainably
managed forests.

LOWY INSTITUTE
FOR INTERNATIONAL POLICY

Contents

Acknowledgments

This book began its life in the course of a conversation with Phillipa McGuinness. Such are her powers to inspire that, before I knew it, I had signed a contract that committed me to producing a manuscript in an insanely short period of time.

I could not have hoped to succeed without some powerful prevailing winds.

First was the fact that I have been thinking and arguing about these issues for the best part of twenty years. It's impossible for me to name all of those with whom I've argued, who have told me things I didn't know, who have changed my mind, who have recommended books or trips or contacts. There are all those organisations that asked me to speak on a topic I'd never thought about before, or asked me to sit on a panel with people who thought differently about issues I'd formed views upon. To try to list all of them is beyond my powers of memory or the forbearance of my publisher. I hope they know who they are.

Next were some wonderful, creative, energetic and tireless researchers who kept a steady stream of articles, statistics, searches and reports flowing into the mill. Edwina Lau, Claudia Mangel, Adam Arnold and Jo Bottcher put in huge amounts of work on this project, and never complained about the vague or cryptic requests that would appear at unreasonable hours on their emails.

Then there were those who were prepared to take the time to read drafts to check I wasn't producing complete rubbish. Don Russell, Mark Thirlwell, Andrew Shearer, Malcolm Cook and Julianne Schultz all fitted my drafts into their already crowded schedules, providing feedback, comments and suggestions that greatly strengthened the manuscript.

After the draft was finished, Heather Cam, James Drown and the staff of UNSW Press clicked into action with stunning precision.

Despite the impossible timetable and dozens of other pressing demands and commitments, this book has been a great joy to write. My colleagues at the Lowy Institute have been unfailingly encouraging and supportive. Sheridan, Oskar and Felix at home have had an uncanny knack of knowing when I need to be distracted, and when I need to write or think.

The person I've thought most about in writing this book has been my father. Frank Wesley was born and raised on the crowded, dusty plains of north-central India. He lived and studied in Japan and the United States, and lived the last third of his life in a small town in Queensland. He would have been more surprised than most at the rise of Asia. But then Frank Wesley liked nothing more than to argue over the unusual and the unexpected.

Introduction

Qantas flight 128 leaves at nine o'clock this evening. There are several options for getting to Central Station. You choose one of the small red taxis that circulate the city constantly. At Central, you buy a ticket to the airport and step straight onto the gleaming silver train. As you settle into the plush seats, the Airport Express whispers out of the station, right on time. You will be at the airport in exactly 24 minutes. High-rise apartments, docks, mountains and bays flash past the windows. This train may not be as fast as Shanghai's magnetic levitation train, which tops 500 kilometres per hour, but it's pretty quick. The airport is as clean and efficient as the train. Check-in, passport control and security are brief delays. Passengers board and the plane leaves right on time.

Next morning, you land half an hour later than scheduled, due to airport congestion. There's a further delay on the tarmac as you wait for the arrival of an operator of the boom walkway. Passport control lines are long; the wait for your bags even longer. Then there are the endless, noisy, disordered queues to get through customs. The line for taxis sends you down to the airport railway station instead – and into another queue for tickets. The train, when it arrives, is dirty and battered. The filthy blue vinyl seats are covered in graffiti, the floor with dirt and newspapers. You crawl towards the city through blackened tunnels and past overgrown retaining walls. It's hot but there's no air conditioning. The train stops for a long time just outside of Central Station, reason unexplained, before limping its way to the platform.

From Central to Central it's taken twelve hours. An international trip by definition takes you from one world to another, but the contrast this time comes as a shock. Last night you were in Hong Kong, a crowded peninsular city with no assets other than its harbour and its seven million people; a city that has been invaded, claimed and counter-claimed five times over the past two centuries, which only a couple of generations ago was dominated by vast, stinking refugee camps periodically devastated by mud slides; a city now of gleaming, ostentatious success, booming energy and disciplined precision. This morning you're in Sydney, a sprawling metropolis of four million; at its mouth a glistening natural harbour; at its back a vast, richly endowed, continent; a continent ruled by the same culture and style of government for the past 200 years, never the subject of hostile claims or invasion; a continent sparsely populated by people who have always been counted among the world's most wealthy, who have just lived through two of the most prosperous decades in their history.

An inversion of our world has happened without us noticing. Australians have traditionally thought of Asia as poor, backward and unstable. When, or if, they went to Asia, they were used to leaving clean, sunlit streets, the latest technology and infrastructure, ubiquitous safety and prosperity, for an adventure among shabby high-rises, roiling street markets and exotic rural scenes. That Asia still exists. But another Asia has emerged, an Asia that showcases the future in the same way that America used to; an Asia that builds infrastructure with an ease that appears beyond our capacities here in Australia; an Asia through whose streets flows wealth that is eye-popping to Australians who have grown up thinking they lived in the rich, lucky country. This new, disconcerting Asia is advancing quickly, past its original isolated islands of progress in Japan, Hong Kong and Singapore. The new Asia is sprouting up in Bangalore, Shanghai, Seoul, Kaohsiung, Kuala Lumpur, Chongqing. The old, reassuring Asia is in retreat.

We've known about Asia's rise for decades. Japan's economy was accelerating away from Australia's in the 1950s, even while we were growing strongly ourselves. Japan, along with Korea, Taiwan, China and the countries of South-East Asia, has accounted for two thirds of Australia's trade for a quarter of a century. And up until now, the significance of Asia's rise for Australia has only been to make us richer and safer. But there are good reasons to suspect that the significance of Asia's continued rise will be less unambiguously positive for Australia. The years ahead will see the emergence of major centres of economic, political, strategic and cultural power that are outside the rules and roll-calls we've become used to. The past quarter of a century has seen Asia's rise simply add to the ranks of the rich and significant countries. The next quarter of a century will see Asia's rise completely overturn the patterns of wealth and significance in the world.

The effects of such a turn of events on Australia would seem to be obvious – but they're not. 'The rise of Asia' is a slogan used extensively in our national conversations, but rarely is it interrogated further than its effects on our own prosperity and safety. My purpose in the following pages is to ask what the rise of Asia will mean for Australia in the coming years. How will the continent to our north, which will inevitably become the centre of world affairs, to which we are inexorably drawn through ties of trade, investment and security, look by the middle of this century? Where will the dangers lie? Where can we find reassurance and safety? What will be the opportunities? And how are we currently placed to make the most and avoid the worst of the new world that is emerging?

Although this book is about looking forward, it looks at Australia's and Asia's future through the lens of the last twenty years. The years between 1990 and 2010, which Allan Gyngell, the head of Australia's peak intelligence agency memorably called 'the transmillennium decades', offer a rich prism through which to view Asia's future and Australia's prospects. These two decades have been arguably the most prosperous years in our national history, and have seen Australia open up to the world as never before. But beyond our shores, the transmillennium has been a period of sudden and remarkable change in Asia's – and the world's – biggest countries, changes so large and fast that they have shifted decisively the way the world works.

Each of the chapters in the book is oriented around a question. Chapter 1, 'Australia rising', begins at home, asking what the past twenty years of extraordinary productivity and prosperity, of internationalisation and internationalism, have meant for Australia's role in its region and in the world. Australia's size and significance, whether it's a 'middle power' able to 'punch above its weight', a price-maker or price-taker, has been a perennial topic of discussion and debate. Against this backdrop Australia has enjoyed twenty years of growth, strength and success that have outstripped all of the countries that it has regularly compared itself with. Through the transmillennial decades, Australia seemed to come of age, shrugging off calamities that kneecapped other countries and used to drag it down too. It was a time of new activism to shape the world around Australia to its own interests and preferences. The transmillennial decades have built a rich, confident Australia to launch into the next two decades.

'The great convergence' (Chapter 2) looks out to our north to ask how sustainable and significant are the rise of Asia's biggest countries. The evidence of the past twenty years shows that the growth rates of the continent-sized economies to our north will remain strong for decades, with increasingly profound effects on the world economy. The dynamo that has produced such extraordinary expansion so far will continue to drive growth into the future. It is the liberation of the productivity, hopes and expectations of hundreds of millions of people by the twin forces of globalisation and moderately pragmatic, sensible government that no longer believes the way to economic success lies in its own hands. The sheer numbers of people, starting from deep poverty but with evidence all around of others' success, is the most powerful enrichment dynamo the world has ever seen. Australia's transmillennial boom looks quite a bit less impressive against the backdrop of the contemporaneous transformation in Asia.

Chapter 3, 'The geometry of power', looks forward to ask how an Asia dominated by wealthier, more powerful countries will look. It begins from a belief that the current scenarios for thinking about Asia's future – most of which rely on models from the past – are simplistic and misleading. The oldest of these theories is that as four or five 'great powers' arise and compete, twenty-first century Asia will start to look much like eighteenth-century Europe. In this world, Asia's great powers will build and maintain a complex and subtle balance among themselves, intriguing, demarching, and skirmishing constantly to ensure none of them becomes all-powerful. A slightly different take skips forward to nineteenth-century Europe, arguing that so dangerous will this balance become that Asia's great powers should settle on a 'Concert of Asia' to collectively manage their rivalries, much as Metternich and Castlereagh stitched together at the Congress of Vienna. Yet another prediction is that Asia will revert back hundreds of years, to a hierarchy of tribute and forbearance centred on the Middle Kingdom. Others again look back only to the Cold War, to suggest that two superpowers – 'Chimerica' – will compete and collude and shape the rest of the world around their pivotal relationship. But a close look at the complex dynamics of power that have already emerged during the transmillennial decades shows how inadequate these models are. 'The geometry of power' argues that no Asian state will open up the sort of power lead that will enable it to convert the region and the world into either a duopoly or a hierarchy. Their growing dependence on the global economy means they will not have the elbow room to play elegant games of balance and skirmish without threatening the entire bases of their stability and prosperity. And the overlapping strands and types of power that overlay Asia mean that not even the most assiduous conducting of a concert of nations will be able to manage such a fluid and fast-evolving power dynamic.

The next chapter, 'The psychology of power' examines another reason why Asia's future will not look anything like Europe's past – or for that matter anything like Asia's past. A closer look at the countries of Asia shows just how their view of themselves and the world is shaped by the profoundly hierarchical nature of their societies. Theirs is a worldview that makes civilisational rivalries enduring and meaningful to how these countries interact as they become stronger and richer. Their hierarchical understanding of the world also made sure that the period of European colonialism experienced by most of them has had deep and enduring effects. With new power comes renewed demands for appropriate respect and influence, and a chafing dissatisfaction with those elements of the way the world works that exclude them, criticise them, or remind them of the time when they were ruled by Europeans, Americans and Japanese. At the same time, Asia's rising giants are in the uncomfortable situation that they are in fact the greatest beneficiaries of a world that they find chafing and unjust. These cross-cutting and contradictory rivalries and neuralgias in Asia further complicate the power picture sketched out in the previous chapter. It means that no settled alliances or power hierarchies will be acceptable to all of the countries of Asia. Their suspicions and rivalries will add a layer of complication to their interests and strategies, making the picture much more nuanced and contingent than we've seen in the past.

Chapter 5, 'Insular nation', returns the story to Australia, looking inside the mind of a country that has just lived through a charmed double-decade of riches, openness and increasing safety. It finds a nation of insular internationalists, well aware of the world and its importance to Australia, but not particularly interested in the transmillennial shifts that are occurring around them. Laying Australia on the therapist's couch, this chapter tries to diagnose why its people are so complacent about how their country relates to the world, so incurious about how the world is changing, and so unprepared to think about how all of this will affect them. Ultimately the world has continued to enrich and reassure Australians with little or no attention or effort on their part. They've ignored the advice of the early 1990s – that to cope with Asia, Australians need to change – but they've prospered anyway. They're used to lucky events averting disaster and to thinking that they're too far away to be affected and too small to matter to the world.

Finally, 'Here comes the world' (Chapter 6) draws all of the trends attending the rise of Asia together into a set of choices for Australia. It returns to Asia's rising giants to ask what their preferences are likely to be, what capabilities they are likely to have, and how they may, or may not, be able to shape the world around them according to their needs and predilections. It is more likely than not that Asia will be a very crowded stage, where sudden and dramatic movements can have unpredictable and unwanted consequences. Even as they grow stronger and richer, they are likely to confront the tar-baby nature of their own strength – with each attempt to flex their muscles and demand their prerogatives comes an immediate reaction from the smaller countries around them in ways that constrain or isolate the giants. But for all the caution this may breed, it will not guarantee another sixty years of safety and wealth for Australia. It is more likely than not that Australia's old beliefs and formulae for dealing with the world will become rapidly obsolete. The world that once seemed so far away and so hard to influence will come much closer, as a new Indo-Pacific power highway solidifies down Asia's eastern coast, veers left just off Australia's northern coast, and curves west towards the Persian Gulf. This world will no longer reward Australians with little effort on their part. As Australia is drawn into the new competition around rivalries and offsetting alignments, the twin oars of its foreign policy – the alliance and multilateral institutions – will no longer bite as deeply into the water. Australia is entering a strange new world, a world for which it is nowhere near psychologically or attitudinally prepared.

*

There Goes the Neighbourhood is an attempt to set out a problem in as clear a set of propositions as possible. Australia is a country that has grown rich from opening itself to the world as never before, but this very process has made it insular and complacent about the world. Asia, the region that holds its future well-being in its hands, is changing far more quickly than Australians are aware of, with consequences they haven't even begun to imagine. This is a book that is long on questions and short on answers. My answer to its questions is simple but hopefully not simplistic: wake up! There are complexities and challenges here that are greater than any we've had to deal with in our history. They are further outside our established routines, expectations and historical models than any we've had to deal with before. And if we're to meet these challenges as a country, the first step is to start taking them seriously. Here is a reform agenda more pressing and consequential than any domestic policy reform we face. How much better will we be at responding if we start thinking about our regional future now, rather than at the point when the new world to our north suddenly imposes its first uncomfortable choice upon us?

1

Australia rising

Friday, 26 January 1990 was a morose Australia Day. The weather in Sydney and Canberra was sullen and close, and storms threatened Brisbane. These were the only capitals which celebrated that Friday, because Victoria, South Australia, Tasmania and Western Australia refused to move the traditional Monday public holiday to a Friday. The prime minister made a half-hearted call for all Australians to celebrate on the same day, while a couple of eminent historians advocated moving it to two completely different dates. That year, more foreigners than Australians were awarded the nation's highest honour, the Companion of the Order of Australia. The flags that Sydney schoolchildren waved were prominently marked 'US Patent No. 4590883'.

Australians had little to be buoyant about. All of the signs pointed towards another recession – and a bad one at that. Interest rates stood at 17 per cent, and Australians' mortgage repayments had climbed 28 per cent in the previous year. People in economic distress had driven up calls to 24-hour crisis lines by over 400 per month. The flagship company of Alan Bond, the entrepreneur who had most embodied the 1980s spirit of Australian audacity and confidence, went into receivership, along with many others. Failed financial institutions littered the legal landscape: the State Bank of Victoria, the State Bank of South Australia, the Teacher's Credit Union of Western Australia, the Pyramid Building Society, the merchant banks Tricontinental, Rothwell's and Spedley's, the Estate Mortgage Trust, and the Order of the Sons of Temperance friendly society. Two of the big four banks had haemorrhaged money and needed to be recapitalised.

In the first week of 1990, Moody's downgraded Australia's credit rating; Standard and Poor's followed within a few days. A fortnight later market researchers Dunn and Bradstreet registered a record slump in business confidence. The Institute of Applied Economic and Social Research reported the lowest levels of consumer sentiment ever recorded. The Australian dollar fell by 6 per cent in the week leading up to Australia Day, despite the Reserve Bank's efforts to prop up its value. On the day before Australia Day, Newspoll recorded that 30 per cent of respondents believed their economic situation would worsen over the next six months, while just 18 per cent thought theirs would improve.

The pessimists were right. By the September quarter of 1990 the Australian economy had slid into a deep downturn. During the recession, the Australian economy shrank by 1.7 per cent, resulting in $30 billion in lost output. By January 1991, the share market had fallen 32 per cent. Commercial property prices collapsed by over 50 per cent. Australia's net foreign debt ballooned to $150 billion by late 1992, or nearly one-third the size of Australia's national output. Australia's payments to service the debt were almost a quarter of the size of all export revenue, the highest level of any developed economy. The economy shed 300 000 jobs, almost doubling the unemployment rate to 10.8 per cent. Between August 1989 and August 1993 the number of long-term unemployed tripled, with people out of work for twelve months or more comprising one-third of all unemployed.

The 1990s recession was even harder to take because it brought to a sudden end a period of economic exuberance and national confidence. The second half of the 1980s had seen the Australian economy growing strongly, at annual rates of over 5 per cent before the end of the decade. It was a time of national pride and sporting success, when a new nationalism infused film and popular music. The spirit of optimism and enterprise was embodied by photogenic and ostentatiously successful entrepreneurs such as Alan Bond and Christopher Skase. Ordinary Australians followed suit, buying property, cars and boats, and taking regular overseas holidays. By the end of the 1980s, domestic consumption was growing by 8 per cent, and Australians' tastes were decidedly cosmopolitan, driving up imports by 29 per cent a year.

As the bad news hit in the 1990s, it was hard not to feel helpless. Just as had happened in 1974 and 1982, when the world economy plunged it took Australia with it. It was little consolation that 10 of the world's 18 developed countries were even harder hit. All of the ebullience of the 1980s looked hollow. It seemed that Australia's was a minor economy whose fortunes were ultimately determined by the world beyond its shores, rather than by effort and enterprise at home. Almost a decade of economic reforms designed to make the Australian economy more flexible and entrepreneurial seemed to have made little difference. The architect of the restructuring, Paul Keating, had warned Australians in May 1986 that unless such reforms were made, 'we will just end up being a third rate economy ... a banana republic'.

Keating's warning had struck a raw nerve in the community at the time because it played to a deep pessimism about the country's long-term economic vitality. At the end of the nineteenth century, Australians had been the wealthiest people on earth, with a per capita income higher than any other society's. But for nearly a century, other countries had been striding confidently past Australia. Even during the long boom years of the 1950s and 1960s, when Australia's per capita growth was consistently over 3 per cent a year, it still lagged behind the average growth rate measured across all developed economies. During the downturns in the 1970s and 1980s, the Australian economy had plunged further and faster than most other wealthy economies, and by the end of the 1980s Australians' per capita wealth was lower than it had ever been when compared to the developed country average.

If Australians had been able to predict events beyond their shores in the twenty years after Australia Day in 1990, they would have been even more pessimistic. Those decades saw a serious financial meltdown somewhere in the international economy every two years. Beginning in 1991, Australia's largest trading partner, Japan, would enter a decades-long period of stagnation, registering growth rates of less than 1 per cent and stumbling through four recessions. Within eight years the other dynamic Asian economies that bought the bulk of Australia's exports, plunged into the region's greatest ever economic crisis, wiping off between one-quarter and one-half of the value of the bourses of some of Asia's fastest growing economies. The following year, 1998, American bond markets ground to a standstill. America also dragged much of the world into recession three times in the first decade of the twenty-first century, as the 'dot-com' bubble burst in 2000, in the aftermath of the September 11 attacks in 2001, and with the sub-prime crisis of 2007–08.

And the plagues were not just economic. Jihadist attacks killed more Australians in the few years after the turn of the century than had died at the hands of terrorists in the rest of the nation's history. Oil prices quadrupled in real terms, rising further than the first oil crisis of 1973 and as high as during the second oil shock in 1980. The early years of the new century ushered in a new age of pandemic viruses threatening rapid transmission and the possibility of sudden infection and death – SARS, bird flu, swine flu – with potentially disastrous effects on international travel and commerce. The same few years would bring drought of a severity not seen for generations to most of southern and eastern Australia. By 2004–05, Australia was in the grips of a terms-of-trade boom of the same scale as the last one in 1974, which had tipped the economy into nearly two decades of high inflation, low growth and high unemployment.

This collection of challenges would be enough to cause panic to anyone with even a passing knowledge of Australia's economic history. Whenever the global economy had stalled – in 1974, 1982 and 1991 – the Australian economy had contracted further and faster than most other developed countries. Of even greater concern, each of these successive downturns had been deeper than any since the end of World War II. With such previous form, it was odds-on that the succession of Asian and then global economic crises between 1990 and 2010 would cause further economic misery in Australia. Nor was there any reason to doubt that the additional threats of terrorist attacks, ballooning energy prices, pandemic scares and drought would only worsen the effects on Australia's already battered fortunes.

Beautiful numbers

But the catastrophe never came. Australia's economy began rising in September 1991, and it has never stopped. Over the next two decades, the Australian economy tripled in size. The annual growth rate of Australia's gross domestic product averaged 3.25 per cent, never slipping beneath 2.5 per cent between 1992 and 2008 and topping 5 per cent in 1998. On a per capita basis, Australia's GDP increased by 182 per cent in the two decades after 1990. All of the chronic problems that had plagued the economy since the 1970s simply vanished. Inflation, which had averaged 8.5 per cent a year during the 1980s, fell to an annual average of 2.6 per cent between 1991 and 2008. The unemployment rate more than halved between 1993 and 2008, from 10.6 per cent to 4.2 per cent. Australians had become used to their economy being talked about with furrowed brows; by the end of the 1990s, Nobel laureates were dubbing it the world's 'miracle economy'.

There was more magic behind the numbers. The economy boomed not only because more Australians were working, but because they were also working more effectively. The 15 years after 1991 saw Australia's productivity increase at an average of close to 2 per cent each year, a rate consistently higher than throughout the previous four decades. The productivity revolution was the result of the 1980s and 1990s economic reforms, which had delivered low inflation and more competition, as well as the fast uptake of new information and communications technologies. These new technologies were especially beneficial because they helped solve stocking and logistics problems, fragmented markets and limits to competition that had hitherto constrained the small, internally dispersed Australian economy. The greater efficiency of the economy delivered a range of benefits: better wages and conditions without offsetting inflation; higher profits for companies and shareholders;

better quality products at reasonable cost; and greater revenues for government.

Australia's growth rates after 1991 were not just extraordinary by the country's own historical standards, they were remarkable in comparison to the performance of other developed countries. Between 1990 and 2008, the Australian economy grew at an average rate of 3.26 per cent a year, compared to an average of 2.6 per cent across all developed economies. It easily out-paced the United States, which averaged 2.8 per cent across the same period, Britain at 2.35 per cent, New Zealand at 2.71 per cent, Japan at 1.44 per cent, Germany at 1.91 per cent, and France at 1.88 per cent. Only a handful of smaller economies bettered Australia: Ireland, Korea, Israel and Luxembourg. Australia's per capita growth was consistently half a per cent higher than both that of the United States and the average of all other developed economies – which were themselves undergoing economic boom times. Australia had not experienced these sorts of leads over other comparable economies since the Korean War. From the 1950s, Australians had become used to being outperformed by other developed economies. In per capita growth terms, Australia had averaged the best part of a whole percentage point behind the rest of the developed world since the 1960s: 3.2 per cent compared to an average of 4 per cent in the 1960s; 1.7 per cent compared to 2.3 per cent in the 1970s; 1.5 per cent to 2.1 per cent in the 1980s. But in the 1990s that percentage point lag became a lead: Australia's average per capita growth sped along at 2.4 per cent a year, the developed world's at just 1.7 per cent.

Australia excelled at more than just growth. Whereas at the end of the 1960s its barriers to international trade and investment were the highest in the developed world, by the 1990s they were the lowest. As a consequence, levels of trade and investment as proportions of the national economy returned to levels not seen since the beginning of the twentieth century, after plumbing historic lows in the 1960s. During the 1990s, the productivity growth rates of Australian workers surpassed the average of workers in other developed economies for the first time ever. Partly as a result of these efficiency improvements, Australia out-performed most other developed economies in keeping inflation to historic lows. And whereas Australians in the early 1990s, with their double-digit jobless rates, had enviously watched America's 'frictional' unemployment rates of around 5 per cent, the flow of envy reversed by 2009. Australia worried about skills shortages with a jobless rate barely topping 5 per cent, while Americans struggled to bring their unemployment under 10 per cent. The spectre of labour and skills shortages drove Australian rates of immigration to their highest levels in decades, and when the Australian population passed 22 million at the end of September 2009, demographers noted that the last million people had been added to the population one year faster than the previous million, and two years faster than the million before that. Whereas between 1901 and 1994 two-thirds of Australia's population growth each year had occurred by the birth of Australian babies, by 2009 immigrants comprised two-thirds of annual growth.

Australia's rise during these transmillennial decades – the twenty years between 1990 and 2010 – was partly a matter of good management. In particular, the raft of economic reforms enacted during the 1980s and 1990s – floating the dollar, opening the capital account, deregulating the financial sector, unilaterally cutting tariffs, implementing competition policy, guaranteeing central bank independence, reforming industrial relations and restructuring the tax system – bequeathed Australia with a more flexible but resilient economic structure for the 1990s and beyond. But the transmillennial boom also benefited from a touch of luck – or more accurately a trifecta. The twenty-years boom was given three successive boosts by three major shifts in Australia's external environment. No other country was in a position to benefit from this trifecta, meaning that

Australia's superior performance after 1991 came partly from being in the right place at the right time.

The lead horse in the trifecta was the structural shift in the global economy that occurred in the early 1990s. By the end of the 1980s, the importance of manufacturing to international trade was falling fast, and the importance of services to production, consumption and trade was increasing at the same rate. This long-term shift underpinned a surge of growth in the global economy by reducing the tendency for wild swings in output and consumption. This taming of volatility was also assisted by the simultaneous control of inflation across developed economies, which reduced their need to periodically slow economic growth to fight it. Global growth in the 1990s was further spurred by the arrival and integration of information and communication technologies which lifted efficiency and integration in Australia and other developed economies. And at the same time as these technologies were boosting productivity, their price was falling fast; between 1990 and 2010, the average prices of information and communications equipment fell by more than 90 per cent. Australia's strong growth and sustained low inflation during the early 1990s rode partly on the back of a horse named global growth.

The second horse was another long-term shift in the global economy: the emergence of Asia as the centre of growth and dynamism. For much of its history, Australia has been remote from the centres of global production and finance, with real consequences for the growth potential of its economy. According to the calculations of the Federal Treasury, until the 1970s only about 16 per cent of world production was located within 10 000 kilometres of Sydney. (By contrast, 94 per cent of world production was within 10 000 kilometres of London.) By the end of the 1990s, 28 per cent of world GDP lay within 10 000 kilometres of Sydney. In addition to the now much reduced transport distances, the costs of trade also started to fall. Partly this was the result of innovations in bulk shipping and containerisation, but it also related to a general fall in trade barriers across most economies. As a result, trade became much more important to the Australian economy, rising from lows of around 28 per cent as a proportion of the economy in the 1960s to 42 per cent by the end of the century.

The second horse brought the third in its wake. By the early years of the twenty-first century, most developed economies had already absorbed the boost from the rise of services and the arrival of the information and communications revolution and were settling into more sedate growth rates. But as Australia's first horse tired, its third hit its straps. In the years after the turn of the century, when everyone in the West was worrying about shadowy networks of terrorists, China began to reshape the world economy. After 2000, China's exports grew on average by 25 per cent each year. By 2008 it was selling seven times more on world markets than it had been in 1999, and twenty-three times more than in 1990. Forests of factories across China's southern and eastern provinces began churning out consumer goods at a rate that would make the rest of the world increasingly dependent on products made in China, while also driving down the prices to all-time lows. But the factory to the world was also transforming itself. As China industrialised, it needed more highways and dams, cities and railways, airports and power stations. A continental-scale economy, China had long been self-sufficient in the materials it needed to build its internal infrastructure. But such was the scale of its demand for minerals, energy, cement and food that China's internal resources were inevitably stretched. The rest of the world had little idea of what was coming.

Primary commodities – food, minerals, energy – had been a 'rust belt' sector since the 1960s. Once Europe and Japan had rebuilt themselves after World War II, the demand for primary commodities slackened. Prices and profits fell, and it became very hard to compete with manufacturing and services – particularly information technology and communications – for the investment needed to build new production. China's commodity hunger took all of two years after the turn of the century to gobble up all of the world market's excess supply of most of the raw materials it needed. Thereafter it began to drive up commodity prices at rates not seen since the Korean War, if ever. Australia became a major supplier of resources to China's rapacious demand because of two unbeatable attributes: the quality and location of its minerals. Australia's iron ore may not be quite as high a quality as Brazil's, but it is a lot closer to China and therefore cheaper to ship; India's and Russia's iron ore may be closer, but theirs is nowhere near the quality of the Pilbara's. It was the same story for an array of other resources, from alumina to zinc. In the years after 2004, the prices of Australia's resource exports increased by 91 per cent, with iron ore prices alone jumping 165 per cent. With falling import prices and a 41 per cent increase in export revenue, Australia's terms of trade lifted by over 70 per cent. The resources boom lifted corporate profits in general by 20 per cent, and contributed 13 per cent to Australia's real GDP during the first decade of the twenty-first century.

All world-beating runs combine good preparation, abundant natural ability, a fair slice of luck – and the capacity to avoid pitfalls. Almost as remarkable as the sheer numbers of Australia's rise was its ability to coast past a dangerous array of events that could have brought it all to a shuddering halt. For the first time in its history, Australia kept growing while either its major trading partners or the rest of the world stumbled into crisis and recession. It did this not once, but three times in 20 years: 1997–98, 2000–01 and 2008–09. Australia avoided the Asian financial crisis because of its floating exchange rate, which maintained the competitiveness of Australian industry and its integration into world financial markets, making it able to restructure its debt in its own currency. The 'dot-com' bust passed Australia by because it made very little information technology equipment. And in 2008, with levels of household debt similar to those of the United States and the United Kingdom, plus a high current account deficit and rising asset prices and credit growth, Australia should have been a prime candidate for infection by the sub-prime crisis. But good luck (a housing boom that had ended in 2003) and good management (a rigorous framework of prudential supervision, strong balance sheets in the major banks, and early action to support liquidity by the Reserve Bank) made Australia one of a select few wealthy countries to escape the crisis. It also helped that Asia's big economies – driven by internal industrialisation, less dependent on foreign investment, and with sheltered financial systems – continued to grow strongly while the North Atlantic economies declined.

There were other squalls that Australia avoided. The early years of the twenty-first century saw over 90 per cent of New South Wales, 65 per cent of Queensland and 48 of 59 Victorian municipalities in severe drought. Agricultural output and exports fell by a quarter, and agricultural income by over 46 per cent. Ordinarily this in itself would have dragged Australia close to recession. But while the drought took almost 1 per cent off economic growth, the Australian economy continued to grow at over 3 per cent during the driest years. The reason is that the farm sector's contribution to the national economy has fallen to around 3.5 per cent, and strong growth in other sectors of the economy masked the drought's effect.

The boom in Australia's terms of trade threatened two different types of pitfall. To those with a sense of history, the China boom affected the Australian economy in a similar way to the terms of trade boom in 1974, which effectively tipped the economy into deep recession and instability. This time, however, a much more flexible domestic economy – particularly due to a floating exchange rate – allowed Australia to absorb the benefits of China's demand without succumbing to the risks. Nor has the increase in the value of the Australian dollar, as a result of high commodity prices, caused other sectors of the economy to contract – the so-called 'Dutch disease' that has hollowed out the economies of other resource exporters. For the best part of a decade Australia's terms of trade boom has seen little contraction in the non-resources or import-competing sectors of the economy.

Striding tall

The story of Australia's transmillennial rise extends beyond mere economic data. In 1990 the country was beset by uncertainty about the wider world. Just months before, the Berlin Wall had fallen, signalling the collapse of the Warsaw Pact and the end of the Cold War that had structured world politics for generations. China had just massacred hundreds of its own students and workers, puncturing hopes for a peaceful global democratic transition. Four years before, New Zealand had been excluded from the ANZUS alliance for refusing to accept visits by American nuclear warships, and in 1987 Australia's defence forces had been humiliated by having to turn back from a mission to intervene in a coup in Fiji. In August 1990, Iraq invaded its neighbor Kuwait, raising real fears of renewed chaos on world oil markets. In 1991, Indonesian troops killed protesters in a cemetery in East Timor, prompting public protests across Australia and threatening to drag Canberra's relations with its largest neighbour to new lows. In protest at the growing trade deficit in the US, Australia's closest ally, beefy congressmen were using baseball bats to publicly smash television sets manufactured by Japan, Australia's largest trading partner. Visiting leaders from some of Asia's booming economies took delight in lecturing Australia over its sluggish economy and indolent workforce, making snide remarks about the 'poor white trash of Asia'. Global trade talks had stalled.

As Europe and North America shored up exclusive economic blocs, and trade tensions rose between Japan and the United States, Asian thinkers and statesmen began talking publicly about a regional association forged between the economies that had boomed by following non-Western 'Asian values'.

Just as Australia remade its fortunes within its borders in the two decades after 1990, so it reshaped its external environment with an influence and impact greater than it had ever wielded. It helped that Australia became a more significant country in the world in the transmillennial decades. Not only did twenty years of consistently strong growth make it a more weighty economy relative to other developed countries by 2010 – the thirteenth largest in the world, and seventh largest developed economy – but its consistently strong performance in growth, productivity, inflation and employment, and its ability to gallop past regional and global calamities made it increasingly noteworthy for the right reasons. In the years after 1990, Australia entered the global economy with greater purpose and impact. Over the next decade several of Australia's iconic brands became global – Qantas, Fosters, BHP, Westfield, News Limited.

A second round of tariff cuts – made during the depths of a recession in 1991 – left the country with some of the lowest trade barriers in the world. By 2000 the country had the lowest barriers to trade and investment of any advanced economy, and as a consequence its trade intensity, or the value of its imports and exports as a proportion of its total economy, had climbed to 42 per cent – up from lows of 28 per cent in the 1960s. In the midst of the commodities boom, Australia was among the world's top five producers of coal, iron ore, aluminium, uranium, lead, zinc, lithium, gold, diamonds, manganese and nickel. At a time of climbing oil prices and mounting concern about energy security, Australia was the world's ninth largest primary energy producer. Australia also became a much more significant force in global financial transactions. By 2006 the flow of capital into Australia was twenty times what it had been in 1992, while the flow of capital out was ninety-five times what it was. Australia had traditionally been a capital importer, but by 2006, the flow of capital out of the country was almost twice as large as that coming in. In 2005 the value of Australian investment abroad was three-quarters as large as the amount of foreign capital invested in Australia. By 2008, the Australian dollar had become the sixth most traded currency on world currency markets. When Asia's economies crashed at the end of the decade it was Australia, matched only by Japan, that stepped in with billion-dollar bailout packages for the three worst-hit economies.

The two decades after 1990 saw Australia engage in an intense burst of diplomatic activism, playing a central role in initiatives that reshaped regional and global architectures. Australian diplomatic activism was catalytic in moving the parties towards an enduring solution to the decade-long war in Cambodia, and an Australian Army general led the peace-keeping force that oversaw peaceful multiparty elections there in 1993. In early 1989, the Australian Prime Minister had proposed a meeting of Asia-Pacific economies as a method of preventing East Asia and North America retreating into competing trade blocs. The first meeting of Asia-Pacific Economic Cooperation (APEC) was held in Canberra in November 1989. Australia pushed for the inclusion of the 'three Chinas' – the People's Republic of China, Hong Kong and Taiwan – in 1992 and ensured that the group's annual meeting was raised to the leader's (as opposed to ministerial) level. Two years later, thanks to vigorous lobbying by Australian Foreign Minister Gareth Evans, the Asia Pacific's own security institution, the ASEAN Regional Forum, held its first meeting. Australian activism in APEC and the Cairns Group, a global caucus of agricultural exporting economies, was a key stimulus in forcing the United States and the European Union to finally agree to a deal concluding the Uruguay Round of global trade liberalisation and to inaugurate the new World Trade Organization. Canberra was also a strong early supporter of the G20, a regular meeting of the finance ministers from the twenty leading economies in the world to discuss global financial stability. Australian diplomats worked hard in the field of nuclear arms control during the 1990s and saw the conclusion of the Comprehensive Test Ban Treaty and the Chemical and Biological Weapons Convention. Between 2002 and 2004, Australian and Indonesian officials managed to organise a regional consultation process on a range of transnational challenges from terrorist financing to people smuggling.

The transmillennial decades also saw Australia flex some strategic muscle following the long lull after the Vietnam War. Two decades of funding increases for the Australian Defence Forces saw Australia achieve the thirteenth highest military spending in the world by 2010. Key acquisitions of air and naval assets reinforced Australia's status as, in the words of strategic analyst Hugh White, the most significant air and naval power south of China and east of India. Australia's armed forces were involved selectively in the first Gulf War of 1990–91 and became steadily more active in the ensuing years. A key turning point was Australia's role in assembling and leading the INTERFET intervention into East Timor in 1999. This was the first time that Australia had led a military intervention, a task vastly more complex and demanding than that of a subordinate coalition partner in an operation led by another country or organisation. Within four years, Australia was assembling and leading a second intervention, this time the RAMSI mission into the Solomon Islands. Even when it wasn't leading, Australia was playing a much more notable role in coalition operations than it had played since 1975. Its contribution to Operation Enduring Freedom, against the Taliban in Afghanistan in 2001–02, was small but effective, with Australian Special Forces making key contributions in that conflict.

The Australian Special Air Service was again a crucial component in the 2003 invasion of Iraq, with Australian air and naval forces also playing active combat roles for the first time since the Vietnam War.

Australia also found itself more closely involved in the great power dynamics of Asia. Its alliance with the United States drew closer after September 11, with key agreements on defence co-operation, intelligence sharing and free trade signed in quick succession. By 2006 there was no ally besides Britain as intimately involved in American operational military planning and intelligence sharing. During the same period, Australia's relationship with China grew steadily closer. Australia became the largest single supplier of iron ore to China after 2001, supplying over 40 per cent of its total imports of iron ore in 2009, and a major supplier of other commodities. Symbolising the new closeness of the relationship, Chinese President Hu Jintao addressed a joint sitting of the Australian Parliament in October 2003, stating that it was a 'key component' of China's foreign policy to consolidate and develop its all-round co-operation with Australia, and that China viewed bilateral ties from a 'strategic and long-term perspective'. The following August, Australian Foreign Minister Alexander Downer, on a visit to Beijing, announced that 'Australia and China would build up a bilateral strategic relationship'. From 2002 Australia also forged security ties with Japan through the Trilateral Security Dialogue, a regular meeting between American, Japanese and Australian officials to discuss security collaboration. In early 2008 Australia and Indonesia signed a major agreement on security co-operation. In December 2008, Tokyo and Canberra signed an agreement to share confidential information, expand joint military exercises and set up regular consultations on disaster prevention, fighting terrorism and peace-keeping. In February 2010 they signed a Defence Acquisition and Cross-Servicing Agreement – the only such agreement signed by Japan other than that with the United States.

It was not just Australian business leaders, politicians, soldiers and officials who strode the international stage during these trans-millennial decades. Australian writers, actors and artists achieved an international prominence in numbers and consistency never seen before. Five Australians – Geoffrey Rush, Russell Crowe, Nicole Kidman, Cate Blanchett and Heath Ledger – won best actor Oscars, two Australian productions won Oscars for best animated film and best short film. Other actors, such as Rachel Griffiths, Anthony LaPaglia, Toni Collette, Naomi Watts and Guy Pierce, played promi-nent roles in global film and television hits. Authors Peter Carey and DBC Pierre were awarded Man Booker prizes for fiction. Austra-lian rock bands such as INXS and Crowded House ranked among the world's top acts in the 1990s. Australians claimed three Nobel Prizes in 1996, 2005 and 2009. In 2009 a global survey ranked Aus-tralia's national 'brand' ninth in the world.

Shaping a generation

A new technology arrived in Australia in the early 1990s: the ability to copy old home movies onto videotapes. It was the ideal Christmas present. Across the country people dug out boxes of Super-8 film, and for the first time in decades sat down with their kids to watch Australian life in the 1950s and 1960s. Most footage was probably much like my family's, dominated by successive family holidays and major occasions, from birthday parties to moving into brand new brick houses. Captured on Super-8 were scenes from a golden age, tanned happy families playing in the surf, sporting exuberant fashions, effortlessly building dream homes and modern suburbs. These were the human faces of Australia's long boom – optimistic, confident, happy. They had little understanding of their parents' view of life, which had been shaped by depression and war. They were buoyed by a baby boom that followed the end of World War II, and their tastes and frontiers were already expanding thanks to the waves of non-British migrants arriving to make new lives in the suburbs. Long-boom Australians' standard of living had improved year on year; they were convinced that the future was going to be even better and that their kids would outdo even what they had achieved. Australians of the early 1990s watching these movies may have laughed at the hairstyles and marvelled at the cheap toll for the Harbour Bridge, but they couldn't avoid the feeling that things were good back then.

The human impacts of Australia's transmillennial boom were as profound and widespread as those of the earlier long boom had been. If future generations become suddenly motivated to watch old digicam recordings, the faces they see will reflect a confidence and optimism similar to that of Australians of the 1950s and1960s. By 2010, Australians were on average almost three times as wealthy as they had been in 1991. Australians' real private wealth increased further and faster in the 15 years to 2006 than it had in the 30 years before 1991. Over that period, real income per capita increased by 40 per cent. Most of this surge in wealth came from the appreciation of assets. Those Australians who had owned property or shares in 1991 saw their value double or triple by 2010. In the first half of the decade after 2000, it was the property boom that drove up wealth; in the second half it was the appreciation of shares. By 2010, household assets in Australia were valued at 8.3 times household disposable income, up from 4.7 times disposable income in 1990. The trans-millennial decades saw a doubling of the number of millionaires in Australia every four years. By 2009 Australia had 174 000 house-holds with investable assets of over US$1 million dollars – the tenth highest number in the world.

But the growth in wealth was not only among the rich elite. Rates of property crime – an indicator of the levels of wealth at the lower end of town – fell steadily after the turn of the century, registering their lowest levels in a decade by 2009. Between 1994 and 2003, the income of the lowest-earning fifth of the Australian population increased by close to 25 per cent, a greater increase than any other income group. This was mainly due to a reduction in unemployment, the growth of real incomes, and the highly redistributive Australian tax system which ensures that the least wealthy 40 per cent of households receive more social benefits than they pay in tax. Yet despite the boost to low-income families, the gap between rich and poor widened. Wealth inequality in Australia reduced between 1994 and 1997, but then began to grow steadily again. According to government statistics, low-income families' share of national wealth declined slightly from 10.8 per cent in 1994 to 10.1 per cent in 2008, while high-income families' share of national wealth increased from 37.8 to 40.5 per cent over the same period.

The effects of the rising wealth of Australians could be seen on the streets of its cities. The two decades to 2010 were a paradise for customers, whose average weekly earnings more than doubled across that period, while they faced only a 70 per cent increase in consumer prices. While Australians' pay packets became steadily thicker, the globalisation of manufacturing pushed down prices on everything from clothes to manchester, white goods to power tools. At the same time, the arrival of internet shopping gave customers more scope than ever before to compare quality and price, and to order direct. Price deflation, coupled with improving quality, was most pronounced in consumer electronics, so when Apple released its 4-gigabyte video-enabled iPod nano in September 2007, it retailed for the same price as the 2-gigabyte model that had been selling for the previous two years. Luxury brands and shop fronts once only seen on trips to Paris, Milan or New York, arrived in strength in all of Australia's capital cities.

The Australian car fleet became noticeably newer and dearer over the course of the transmillennial decades. By 2010, car affordability in Australia was at its highest point in close to 30 years. In that year it took just 31 weeks of average wages to buy a Ford Falcon, compared to 39 weeks in 2000. But while sales of all new passenger cars had increased 50 per cent between 2010 and 1990, sales of luxury cars were nearly five times greater than in 1990. By March 2010, luxury cars constituted almost 6 per cent of all new cars sold in Australia; in 1990 just 1.7 per cent of all cars sold were luxury cars. More four-wheel-drives were bought by Australians in the year to July 2010 than at any other time since such statistics began being collected in the early 1990s. During the transmillennial decades, the confidence and flamboyant spending of the top end of town began to infuse the rest of society. It also helped that Aston Martins, Ferraris, Lambourginis, Porsches, Jaguars, Bentleys, Rolls Royces, Mercedes Benzs and BMWs had also become more affordable: in 2010 it took a worker on average salary 43 weeks to afford a BMW 320i, down from 54 weeks in 2005. The price of a BMW 525i Sport rose just 13 per cent between 2000 and 2010, while real wages rose by 63 per cent. Because of lower tariffs and a stronger Australian dollar, the affordability of luxury cars improved at a faster rate than other passenger vehicles between 1990 and 2010.

With more money to spend and prices of consumer items falling, Australians also began investing more heavily in the property market. While sales of investment properties rose strongly, the main effect was through Australians acquiring or improving the homes they lived in. By 2006, 35 per cent of Australian households were paying off mortgages, compared to 27 per cent in 1996. Whereas in 1990 only one-fifth of Australian homes had four or more bedrooms, one-half of all new houses built between 1994 and 2004 had four or more bedrooms. During the property market's boom years, between 2000 and 2007, the value of dwelling assets in Australia increased by 120 per cent, compared to an 83 per cent increase for other assets. Partly this was the result of booming demand. Between

1985 and 2005, an average of 150 000 homes were built each year; the population increased by an annual average of 240 000. After 2005 the population increased by an average of 480 000 a year, with little change in the number of houses built. Partly the housing boom was also a result of low interest rates and friendly tax laws, but it was also the result of a flourishing property culture, driven by a constant awareness of rising property prices and a government grant to first home buyers, which was premised on, and gave emphasis to, a belief in the centrality of the property sector to the health of the Australian economy. Australian television programs featuring home renovation competitions or working the property market regularly topped the viewer ratings.

The spending and investment behavior of Australians reflected a strong sense of confidence that the good times would continue. The Lowy Institute's annual surveys of Australians' views about the world reveal a steady increase in optimism about Australia's future economic performance, reaching record highs of 86 per cent in 2009 and 2010 – up from 67 per cent in 2005. With greater confidence came a greater willingness to take on debt. By 2010 Australia's total household debt was around $750 billion, or $40 000 per head of population. Whereas in the 1980s, Australian household debt was an average of 45 per cent of total household income; by 2010 it stood at 156 per cent. During the transmillennial decades, Australia went from having one of the lowest debt to income ratios in the developed world to having one of the highest. This debt was being incurred especially through investment in housing: 89 per cent of all household debt in 2010 was in home loans (62 per cent) or residential investment loans (another 27 per cent). Australians' optimism and willingness to take on debt was driven by the inexorable appreciation of the assets they were borrowing to acquire. By 2007, median house prices were six times what they had been twenty years earlier. The total value of household assets was nearly eight times household income, while total household debt was just 17 per cent of total assets. When household interest payments reached historic highs in December 2007, they were still at only 12 per cent of disposable household income. At that time, the mortgage default rate was less than a third of one per cent, half the rate in 1996.

The growing material comfort and confidence of Australians were reflected in other decisions too. By 2010, young Australians were deferring the decision to settle down – marry, get a 'serious' job, buy a house and start a family – until their late twenties. In 2007, the median age for first marriages was 29 for men and 27 for women, both four years older than they had been twenty years earlier. The boom (and doting baby-boomer parents) freed Australia's youth to undertake tertiary study, travel, join bands and promote social causes during their twenties, without worrying about the pressures of income or responsibility. Seven million Australians ventured overseas in 2009, twice the number of travellers in 1999. By the mid-1990s, Australians' levels of educational attainment passed the average for developed countries for the first time since these statistics were collected. The first decade of the twenty-first century also witnessed a mini baby boom. When Australia reached its lowest ever birth rate of 1.7 babies per woman in 2001, many demographers predicted declines to 1.5, such as were occurring in European countries, by the end of the decade. Instead, fertility surged by over 10 per cent, to 1.97 babies per woman, with 2009 seeing the highest number of births ever recorded in Australia (just under 300 000). This occurred at a time when the proportion of Australian women choosing not to have children rose to historic and comparative highs (nearly one quarter), meaning that a significant source of the increase was that couples were choosing to have more children – three or four instead of the previously customary two. With comfort and confidence came a new concern with quality of life as 'sea changers', over three-quarters of them younger than 50, migrated out of the big cities to the temperate, coastal climates of South-East Queensland and central-northern New South Wales. Between 2003 and 2009, half a million people moved into South-East Queensland.

*

Everyone knows the feeling when, for that most fleeting moment in a game, an event, a situation, everything goes right. When every serve goes in, every cast gets a bite, each remark is appropriately profound or hilarious, when even the wildly unlikely becomes effortlessly possible. These rare and brief episodes are accompanied by their own psychological state, certainly of profound exhilaration, but also of wonder – and dread that it will all come to an end, returning us to the mediocre, random life we usually live. The transmillennial boom has had material effects on Australia which can be counted, measured and listed. But it couldn't fail to have had a psychological effect also. The good times shape people and societies as profoundly as the bad times. Just as the psychological effects of the 1970s and 1980s shaped the story of the two decades after 1990, so Australia's experience of the transmillennial boom will shape the attitude with which it faces the second and third decades of the twenty-first century. But before looking at these effects, we need to see how the countries to our north fared during the transmillennial decades.

2

The great convergence

In the rankings of achievement and impact per head of population, it is hard to go past Sweden. A nation of just 9 million people is responsible for a slew of global icons: H&M, Tetrapak, Volvo, Ikea, Bang and Olufson, Saab, Ericsson. Each of these great Swedish brands is renowned for its design, and all but the first for superior quality engineering. Design and engineering services and products make up over half of the Swedish economy, and half of Sweden's exports. It is no coincidence that this is the nation that created the most prestigious annual awards for achievement in the sciences – the Nobel Prize.

So for those who were paying attention, the news that broke in December 2009 came as a shock. Sweden and Norway had been considering which telecommunications company they would entrust with rolling out a next generation mobile telephone and broadband network across much of Scandinavia. Most observers assumed it would be one of Scandinavia's global brands – either Sweden's Ericsson or Finland's Nokia – although there was an outside chance that another European or even an American company would win the contract. Since the late 1980s, global mobile telephony had been dominated by American and European firms: Alcatel, Ericsson, Motorola, Nokia, Nortel and Siemens. They controlled the intellectual property and determined the standards and guidelines for developing mobile telephony networks. But in December 2009 the governments in Stockholm and Oslo decided on a company few had even heard of: Huawei Technology. It was based not in Europe or North America, but in Shenzhen, China. Huawei – which means 'China is great' – began life with just 14 employees in a small office in a crowded street in Shenzhen, the original 'Special Economic Zone' created by Beijing as a localised and contained hot-house for experimenting with market-based economics.

Huawei was the creation of Ren Zhengfei, a 34-year-old former colonel in China's People's Liberation Army who had been director of its Information Engineering Academy. With the help of a small loan and some contacts in the military, Ren's company began importing telephone switching equipment and PBXs into China from Hong Kong.

But as China opened up to the world, powerful global competitors were entering this market. Ren gambled everything on designing Huawei's own switching equipment. His engineers designed a telephone exchange system able to accommodate five times the number of switchboards as those of his competitors – and the company prospered. Huawei's success was not just a matter of design but of strategy. With China globalising, the competition for market share was white hot. Ren's military training had been heavily steeped in the strategic doctrine of Mao Zedong: encircle the cities by winning the countryside. Huawei avoided going head to head with the international heavyweights moving into China's major cities, instead concentrating its resources on rural areas and minor cities. Where the major players would send a handful of salesmen into the countryside, Huawei sent hundreds. In a rare interview with a Western consultant, Ren described Huawei as imbued with a 'wolf spirit' – a sensitive nose, aggression and persistence in attack. By the early 1990s, Huawei was one of a handful of emerging, hungry Chinese telecommunications companies.

It was a handy profile to have. In 1992 Beijing decided that China would become a leading player in the global telecommunications and information technology sector. To be a passive customer of the foreign technologies spearheading the information technology and communications revolution was not only a blight on the nation's pride, it would also cede permanent dominance in telecommunications systems and information security to the rich Western nations that already held most of the levers of power in the global economy. Accepting the standard network architectures developed by the Europeans and Americans would make Chinese companies permanent price-takers, compelled to design their own systems on others' specifications while paying royalties for the privilege. A nationwide research project was launched in 1992, with the aim that China would produce its own technology for the next generation of mobile telephony. By 1998 China had presented its own second generation mobile telephone system for registration with the International Telecommunications Union (ITU). Two of its leading communications companies – ZTE and Huawei – were key collaborators in this effort. In June 1998 the ITU accepted China's architecture, called TD-SCDMA, as one of three global mobile telephony transmission standards.

Being a leading telecommunications company in China brought favourable treatment from Beijing. Huawei was regularly the recipient of generous research grants from the government. When Huawei was ready to launch into the international market, it was extended a US$10 billion line of credit by the China Development Bank and a US$600 million loan from China's Export-Import Bank. Such success also brought a range of eager suitors from among the global telecommunications leaders, anxious to get a market advantage in an economy whose telecommunications sector grew almost three times as fast as the rest of the economy for the twenty years after 1990. So Huawei and other Chinese companies signed agreements with global icons – Seimens, Nokia, Ericsson, Samsung – and enlisted them in developing China's own TD-SCDMA standard.

The success of his first gamble convinced Ren of the necessity of constant innovation in research and design. In the early years, Huawei probably resorted to the reverse engineering and copying of leading technologies (Cisco Systems and Fujitsu took or threatened legal action) but it then began to innovate on its own. The company devotes 10 per cent of its profits to research and development. By 2009 the company employed over 40 000 design engineers in six cities in China, as well as Stockholm, Dallas, Silicon Valley, Bangalore, Ferbane and Offaly in Ireland, Moscow, Jakarta, and Wijchen in the Netherlands. Huawei's research and development division is the most prestigious and best-paid in the company – and also the largest, comprising almost half of Huawei's workforce. It is pervaded with a highly competitive culture of inducements and rewards, as well as the constant threat of being among the 5 per cent of least productive employees sacked annually. Huawei has taken out over 20 000 patents for new technologies.

As signs emerged that the Chinese market was cooling, and as telecommunications deregulation rippled across the globe, Huawei decided to expand internationally. Once again, Ren remembered his Mao – or more accurately his Lin Biao. In the 1960s, Marshall Lin, Mao's chosen successor, applied people's war to the world stage: the cities (the developed West) would be taken after the world revolution first dominated the countryside – the developing world. With a vigour that would have made Lin Biao proud, Huawei launched into the developing world: the former Soviet Union and Eastern Europe, Africa, Latin America, and the Middle East. As the dominant international players competed with each other to develop and market cutting-edge equipment, in these developing markets Huawei opted for 'good enough' technology – devices and services that were basic and reliable but cost from a third to a half less than the premium offerings. Often there was a helping hand from Beijing, such as when Nigeria was loaned US$200 million to help it establish a mobile telephone infrastructure – supplied by Huawei. By 2006, 65 per cent of Huawei's sales came from outside China – and more than 90 per cent of these were in developing country markets.

The year 2000 brought the 'dot-com' crisis, a plunge brought on by the realisation that information and communications technology were available in limitless supply with ever-increasing sophistication and prices – but ultimately facing finite demand. The other big telecommunications companies were hit just as hard as computer and internet-based concerns. As its major European and American rivals were distracted by painful restructuring, Huawei now moved into the developed markets. It relied heavily on its price competitiveness, with prices so low that its competitors wondered how it was possible for Huawei to make a profit. Rather than mount an expensive brand recognition campaign among consumers, it sold its products as 'white label' technologies – manufactured by Huawei but carrying the brands of better-known mobile telephone companies. The strategy was not to capture the consumer but the local telecommunications company. In a fractured market, Huawei promoted itself as one of the few vendors in the world able to provide end-to-end third-generation mobile telephony products – from transmission infrastructure to mobile handsets. In 2005 Huawei was selected by British Telecom as the preferred supplier of its twenty-first century network strategy, and it signed a global framework strategy agreement with Vodafone for mobile network infrastructure. In 2006 Motorola signed a deal to distribute and install Huawei equipment, and Germany's Versatel contracted Huawei to build its new fibre optic network. In 2007 France Telecom selected Huawei to supply equipment for its third-generation mobile telephone network. By 2009, Huawei had 31 of the world's top 50 telecommunications companies as clients, and was the world's second-largest supplier of mobile telephony equipment, behind Sweden's Ericsson. By July 2010, Huawei had made it to the Fortune 500 list, with annual sales of US$21.8 billion and net profits of US$2.76 billion.

Divide, then multiply

The emergence of Huawei is startling because it challenges layers of preconceptions that have built up over generations about how the world works. As basic as state borders are to our mental maps of the shape of the world is an awareness of the huge variation in wealth and living standards between human societies. An entire intellectual cottage industry has emerged to offer explanations for the wealth gulf, and to suggest ways of reducing or eliminating it. All of these analyses are built on a single assumption: that the trajectory of Western societies over the past 200 years is the standard against which the performance gap of other societies is measured. The misfortunes of those other societies are then traced to something that the West had but they lacked – from Protestantism to geography to a peculiar flair for exploitation. The remedy seemed therefore fairly straightforward: to close the wealth gap between nations, all you had to do was to make sure the others copied the West in certain key areas. It was that simple.

Except – it wasn't. As the colonies of the West gained independence, they had no shortage of help and advice on how to develop advanced economies. Global and regional institutions such as the World Bank and the Asian Development Bank were founded and funded, great research projects embarked upon, and armies of Western volunteers and development experts sent into the field to provide targeted, practical advice and funds to speed the development process. Despite all the ideas and idealism, the money and the engineering, the results were not impressive. One success was that a 'green revolution' in agricultural science had lifted crop yields and averted the cycles of serious famine in Asia and Africa. But beyond alleviating hunger, the development performance of the former colonies was anaemic. Stuttering progress was repeatedly reversed as world commodity markets plunged or during cycles of political instability and mismanagement.

By the 1970s, an attitude of pious resignation settled over Western societies. The backwardness of the ex-colonies was congenital. They were collectively named the 'Third World' – a designation of exasperation – separated by a huge gulf from the ever-richer First World. If whole Third World economies couldn't be helped there was still a humanitarian obligation to help poor people. Attention shifted to communities, to building sanitation, tackling disease, promoting education. The First World–Third World divide acquired a sense of permanence – a regrettable but inevitable result of the evolution of history. Whereas for centuries the great civilisations of Asia had dazzled the backward societies of Europe with their wealth, opulence, sophistication and learning, they had now lapsed into indolence and squalor just as the light went on in Europe. European societies threw off the shackles of cosmic fatalism and began experimenting with everything from financial organisation to mechanising cloth-making. Economic historians trace to the turn of the nineteenth century two great divides in world economic affairs. At that time Gregory Clark finds a sudden and startling growth in human consumption, wealth and life expectancy among a small number of people in Europe and North America, and a steady decline in these indicators in the rest of humanity. At the same point Angus Maddison and Kenneth Pomeranz traced a marked divergence between societies' share of world population and their contribution to world economic output. In other words, over the space of a few generations around the turn of the nineteenth century, the societies of the West exploded the logics of world economics that had existed for millennia. Not only had a small number of people clustered around the North Atlantic achieved standards of living never before seen in history, but they were suddenly producing the vast bulk of all global economic output.

The peoples of Europe and their settlers had never made up more than one-fifth of all the Earth's people, and until the end of the eighteenth century they contributed about a fifth of global economic activity. With the onset of the industrial revolution in the West, their population climbed slightly, but at nothing like the rate of their productivity. By the 1950s the Europeans, plus their cousins in North America and Australasia, still made up just over 21 per cent of all humans on the planet, but they contributed almost two-thirds of all economic activity. Their story in the two centuries since the industrial revolution was an apparently endless cycle of stability, prosperity, power and production. Theirs were the leading parts on the world's stage; their decisions and disagreements shaped the rest of the world; their observations interpreted the run of history; their preferences aligned and realigned the dreams and possibilities of all on the planet. The three-quarters of humanity not in Europe,

North America, Japan or Australasia were the passive chorus to the lead actors' gambits. For most of history the large populations of Asia's major societies was a sign of their prosperity and their superior organisation and hygiene. They were crowded but industrious. In the eighteenth century the Chinese Empire and the kingdoms of the Indian subcontinent between them ruled over nearly half of the world's people, who produced just over half of the world's economic output. But the passage of the North Atlantic's rise was a story of Asia's decline. By 1975, China ruled over just under one-fifth of the world's people but produced not even one-twentieth of the globe's economic output. India, with only slightly fewer people, was responsible for even less of global economic activity. The peoples of Asia and Africa seemed trapped in a poisonous cycle of instability, incompetence, impoverishment and stagnation.

With this record, for over two hundred years it seemed that the First World would remain first and the Third World last, and never the twain would meet. They assumed the permanence of compass points: the developed 'North' and the underdeveloped 'South'. In 1985, leading international relations scholar Stephen Krasner predicted:

> The gap between Northern and Southern capabilities is
> already so great that even if the countries of the South
> grew very quickly and those of the North stagnated (an
> unlikely pair of assumptions in any event), only a handful of
> developing countries would significantly close the power gap
> within the next one hundred years.

The only exceptions to the seemingly unbridgeable gulf were a few small countries scattered along Asia's eastern coast. After World War II these societies seemed determined to jump the gulf from the Third to First World and to do so quickly. Each of them shared a combination of existential desperation, a lack of land and resources, geopolitical fear and single-minded discipline. First Japan recreated and then surpassed the miracle that followed the Meiji restoration a century earlier; Hong Kong, Singapore and Taiwan followed close behind; and in turn were followed by South Korea. All were in deep strategic alignment with the United States and benefited from its armed might, open markets and free-wheeling finance. Suddenly there were Asian faces among the world's wealthy. But when the novelty wore off, little had changed about the basic shape of the global economy. A small minority still controlled the majority of the world's wealth.

Beyond these 'Asian tigers' still lay the vast, sullen Asian land-mass, the realm of subcontinental civilisations and ancient empires. Here lay nations with populations numbering in the hundreds of millions – a surfeit of humanity living in abject poverty, their vast under-classes clogging the arteries of sluggish economies, multiplying at a rate that swamped the capacity of anaemic growth to provide jobs or welfare. These were vast serried bureaucracies and frameworks of entitlement overlaid by the dead hand of antique traditions. These were regimes given to shrill self-righteous moralising, erratic shifts in policy alignment and sudden border wars. Command economies were built for prestige – nuclear weapons, space programs, heavy industry – while rates of poverty remained stubbornly high. Here was where nearly three-quarters of the world's poor lived.

But then, one after another, it was as if internal alarms started beeping deep inside the governments of these inert giants. Theirs was not a condition of stasis but a trajectory of mounting crisis. The quest for ideological purity, the cycles of state-inflicted turmoil, the quixotic prestige projects had produced not strength but extreme fragility. Their economies were grotesque landscapes of bottlenecks and excess capacity administered by rigid and doctrinaire economic orthodoxies enacted by listless and stifling bureaucracies. The euphoria and optimism of the freedom struggle had dissipated, the ugly reality of poverty had sunk in, and there was little confidence that governments could do anything about it. Such was the sense of crisis that the regimes of these Asian giants were prepared to quietly bury entire philosophies upon which they had built and justified their rule. They began to experiment with market mechanisms at a time when Western market economies were in turmoil, struggling with inflation, unemployment and wild swings of growth and recession. They began to wade into a global economy that they knew had been shaped by a few wealthy societies in their own interests.

*

The first and greatest iconoclast was China. Few countries had fought as long, as hard, or at such great cost for revolutionary purity from backward tradition, external domination and capitalist exploitation as had China. The first ten-year plan promulgated after Mao's death reiterated the priorities of previous plans: a continuation of the collectivisation of agriculture and channelling investment towards heavy industry to increase fertiliser and agricultural mechanisation. But from 1978, China's leaders realised that this would only perpetuate the fate of the majority of the population living in miserable rural poverty, as agricultural production stagnated while the wealth divide between the cities and the countryside widened.

The first reforms were localised, tentative, gradual, and liable to be repealed at the slightest sign of undesirable consequences – as were all of China's liberalisation measures over the next two decades. In remote Anhui province the system of agricultural communes was dismantled in favour of a household responsibility system. Land and equipment were leased to families, who in return were obliged to submit a set amount of their produce to the state before selling the rest on the open market. At the same time the pejorative labels for wealthy peasants and landlords were quietly abandoned. After productivity and prosperity increased markedly in Anhui, the household responsibility system was carefully extended across the country. By 1983 China's agricultural sector had been decollectivised and restrictions on rural industry had been removed. Price reform followed: the careful adoption of a dual system of state sector and private sector prices designed to underpin broader consumer-focused growth in the economy while minimising its inflationary impact. Price reform exposed the inefficiencies of state-owned corporations, providing greater space for flourishing private enterprise, particularly in rural industry and the services sector. The relaxation of restraints on people's internal mobility led to a massive migration from the countryside to the cities, providing a ready labour force for China's new industries.

In China there was no grand plan of liberalisation akin to Russia's shock therapy of the 1990s. Rather there was a slowly growing conviction that emphasising productivity, consumption and raising living standards was the best way of delivering steady, broad-based and long-term growth. The system of national economic planning delivered through direct administrative control was progressively abandoned in sector after sector, and invariably resulted in sudden lifts in productivity. From the earliest years of reform there was an unquenchable eagerness to learn from other countries' successes and failures. Keeping reform and its impacts synchronised and smoothed across such a vast nation was a massive challenge, and China's economy fluctuated wildly during the 1980s and 1990s as the government struggled to master the economic levers. These dilemmas occurred daily, from the national and regional level down to the local. When in the late 1980s Beijing taxi drivers were granted the ability to charge market fares, it provoked outrage and strikes among Beijing's bus drivers who had no such capacity to make profits. By concentrating on rural reforms Beijing was able to reduce the rural–urban divide, but at the expense of relative stagnation in the cities. Ultimately escalating imbalances in fortunes and expectations led to nation-wide protests among urban students and workers in 1989 – and to the massacre at Tiananmen Square.

By the onset of the 1990s, China confronted a choice between pressing ahead with the heady risks of liberalisation or returning to the comfort of command and control. The Tiananmen protests had almost brought down the Chinese Communist Party, while Mikhail Gorbachev's tentative liberalisation in the Soviet Union had resulted in its implosion and the unravelling of the Eastern Bloc. China's two most powerful reformers, Deng Xiaoping and Jiang Zemin, faced off against revisionists led by Chen Yun. The debates were about doctrine as well as outcomes. Jiang related outcomes to doctrine: 'Poverty is not socialism'. Deng's decision to tour the booming southern coastal cities, the epicentres of the new China, signalled not only the triumph of the reformers but their determination to press ahead with further liberalisation. Stock exchanges were opened in Shanghai in December 1989 and in Shenzhen in July 1991. The fourteenth congress of the Chinese Communist Party in 1992 explicitly endorsed the concept of a socialist market economy.

By 2010 the results were clear. The economy was 14 times larger than it had been in 1978, and the average Chinese citizen was 11 times richer. Industrial output had multiplied by a factor of 59 and foreign trade by a factor of 124. In 1978, two-thirds of all Chinese were living on less than a dollar a day; by 2010 fewer than one tenth did so. By September 2010, China had 130 billionaires. In a generation China had become the world's second-largest economy and held the largest hoard of foreign exchange reserves. It was the world's largest trading nation, exporting more each year than all but a handful of economies produced.

*

Vietnam was the next to hear the warning bells. By 1986 the complete failure of Hanoi's collectivisation of agriculture and nationalisation of industry and trade was manifest. It was one of the poorest countries in the world, with stagnating agricultural and industrial production and a rapidly growing population. Year after year it faced acute food shortages and hyperinflation. Thanks to its occupation of Cambodia, it was internationally isolated and saw its aid receipts fall by 50 per cent over the decade to 1986. The onset of Gorbachev's new foreign policy in the Soviet Union meant that Vietnam's staunchest supporter was directing its attention elsewhere. Also in 1986, Le Duan, the great revolutionary leader, died, providing the same space for policy re-evaluation as the death of Mao had in China.

The reformers in Hanoi had watched China's decollectivisation of agriculture closely, and they enacted their own land reform from the last months of 1986. This gave land-use rights to peasant families, turning households into production units with market-based incentives to maximise production. Price reform, combined with fiscal adjustment and monetary restraint, saw inflation fall from 160 per cent in 1988 to under 10 per cent in 2007. State industry was reformed in stages, gradually being restructured, given more autonomy, and encouraged towards commercial operations, while at the same time encouraging the growth of the private sector. Bank liberalisation separated commercial banks from the central bank and put them all on the same commercial footing as joint-stock and private banks. Company and investment law was reformed to boost the market economy, and trade and investment barriers were slashed. By 1990 the growth of the private sector was given legal sanction through the promulgation of the Private Business Law.

The results were less spectacular than in China, but the returns on reform were just as unmistakable. Between 1988 and 2008 the Vietnamese economy grew at an average rate of 7.4 per cent every year. By 2008 the Vietnamese economy was over 14 times its size in

1988. Poverty halved between 1988 and 1998 and continued to fall precipitously over the next decade. The average Vietnamese person was more than ten times as wealthy in 2008 as he or she had been twenty years earlier. In a sign that others were watching what was happening in Vietnam, foreign direct investment into the country quadrupled in the five years to 2008. A nation that had been closed and defensive to the world had become a vigorous trading state, with exports of goods and services worth almost 80 per cent of its entire economy.

*

By the first months of 1991, it was obvious (to anyone who was watching) that India could no longer just 'muddle through'. The early 1980s reforms which had started to open India up to the global economy had not worked as expected. Whereas the Asian tigers had thrived on exports, India found that its hunger for imports far out-stripped its ability to capture export markets. By the late 1980s, as the country's energy thirst grew, domestic oil production began to fade. India slipped further and further into debt, nearly doubling what it owed between 1985 and 1990. It was already a bad posi-tion to be in, but just then the outside world served India a devas-tating one-two combination. In August 1990 Iraq invaded Kuwait, sending world oil prices through the roof and, at the same time, the world went into deep recession, cutting demand for exports by nearly half. With its export markets tanking and its import bill exploding, India's debt went stratospheric. The value of the Indian rupee came under sustained attack. The Reserve Bank of India spent half of the country's foreign exchange reserves defending the value of the currency. Eventually it secured a US$2.2 billion loan from the IMF, using some of India's gold reserves as collateral – which meant airlifting 67 tons of gold bullion to London and Switzerland.

Since Independence from colonial British rule India had never been in such an abject position.

Independent India had been built upon repudiation – of the exploitive excesses of colonial rule, of the free-wheeling spirit of (Western) global capitalism, and of the free-trade ethos of the West. The new independent government decided it would run the economy – steel production and manufacturing, mining and power generation, telecommunications and insurance. Soviet-style five-year plans directed the top end of the economy. Imports were anathema. Whatever foreigners could ship to India, Indians should make themselves – with the massive support of state-owned industry. Competitive industries were clogged with obligations and regulations aimed at employing the poor. Exports were widely seen as a fool's game, a plot by the rich countries to distort and direct the Indian economy. Just to reinforce their belief in themselves as independent India's wisest guardians, the government established a complex and maddening thatch-work of licenses and regulations governing the establishment of private businesses, inadvertently creating a vast system of kickbacks, entitlements and resistance to any form of liberalisation. And in the world's largest democracy, every set of regulations and entitlements soon became ensnarled in a web of patronage and incumbency.

The 1991 crisis brought down the government of Prime Minister Chandra Shekar. The new government of Narasimha Rao knew it had to act quickly or face the same fate. Its immediate priority was to cut external debt. The rupee was devalued quickly, and moved to a floating exchange rate by the end of 1993. The complex mess of licenses and regulations was progressively attacked, with licenses for all but 18 industries abolished by the end of 1991. By the end of the decade a further 12 sectors were dropped from the licensing list. Huge sectors of the economy previously reserved for state control were subjected to new privatisation pressures and incentives. Price controls were steadily abandoned. At the same time, investment was liberalised, removing controls on interest rates and the need for central approval of major loans. Trade restrictions and tariffs were significantly dismantled. 'Special Economic Zones' were introduced to encourage the duty-free import–export dynamism of some sectors of the Indian economy.

The results were quick to appear. An economy which had grown at a feeble 3.5 per cent a year for four decades grew at nearly twice that rate – 6.4 per cent – for the two decades after 1990. India's economy quadrupled in size between 1991 and 2008, picking up speed in the second decade to be two-and-a-half times its 2000 size by 2008. By 2010, *The Economist* was predicting that India's growth rate could outstrip China's within a decade. The average Indian's income increased three-fold between 1991 and 2008. India's trade with the rest of the world, which had fallen to less than 5 per cent of the size of its economy in the early 1970s, had reached almost 25 per cent by 2008. And as India began to rack up investment-grade assessments from credit ratings agencies, foreign money poured in, quadrupling the size of inbound foreign direct investment between 2005 and 2008. Between the late 1970s and 2010, India's poverty rate dropped from over half of its population to just over one-quarter. The United Nations predicted in 2010 that by 2015 India would have halved its 1990 poverty rate.

*

The crisis that hit Indonesia in 1997 seemed to play the Chinese, Vietnamese and Indian experiences in reverse. The Indonesian economy had been growing at an average rate of 7.3 per cent each year since 1990, easily qualifying it as South-East Asia's giant among the tigers. Trade and investment were growing strongly, poverty rates fell from over 40 to just 11 per cent by 1996, and life expectancy increased by 22 years. The Asian crisis reversed these gains within a matter of weeks as capital flooded out of the country. In the year after the crisis hit, the economy halved in size and the rupiah was devalued by 500 per cent against the American dollar. Unemployment and poverty rates doubled. Rioting brought down the Suharto regime, and attacks against ethnic Chinese Indonesians led to their flight to Singapore or Australia – taking their money with them. Sectarian violence flared and Indonesian troops withdrew from East Timor amid terrible carnage that followed a United Nations plebiscite. Jihadist terrorism began a drum-beat of outrage. Diagnoses of the crisis drew the world's attention to the corruption and nepotism endemic in the Indonesian economy. Many predicted Indonesia's complete economic implosion, or disintegration, or both; few expected even a return to slow growth within a decade.

But what happened next in Indonesia was in many ways even more remarkable than what had happened in the other giants: an economic transformation in the midst of the political transformation of a nation gripped by serious ethnic, religious and communal turmoil. An economy that had been downgraded to junk bond status, which had once relied on oil revenues but had now become a net importer, started to grow strongly. True, the growth rates were higher during Suharto's later years but by then the Indonesian economy was seriously distorted by the deep post-Independence biases of the Indonesian elite: economic nationalism, suspicion of Chinese Indonesians and an urge to promote the fortunes of ethnic Malay ('pribumi') Indonesians. The New Order state and military had become deeply entwined with the economy, promoting state industry and import substitution, half ownership of all foreign businesses by Indonesian interests, and a system of patronage through a complex licensing system. The Indonesian economy was dominated by large conglomerates protected by patronage networks centred on the president's family and party. Banks proliferated as capital poured into the country, and finance flowed according to patronage. The shock of the crisis exposed the rotten heart of the system, and as Suharto's power collapsed, Indonesia was hit harder and longer than any of the other crisis-hit economies.

The democratic governments that followed the fall of Suharto moved resolutely to dismantle the legacy of the old regime. Indonesia's political system and economy were extensively decentralised. The military was progressively removed from politics and the economy. The big business conglomerates that had dominated the New Order economy were broken up. One prominent target was the private banks that had financed these big conglomerates, and the banking sector was rationalised and subjected to stronger regulation. The overall economy was liberalised, with barriers to trade and investment progressively reduced, and the systems of regulation and patronage dismantled. As important as the economic reforms were the political and security achievements. Presidents and parliaments were elected in successive elections with high voter turn-out, very low violence or fraud, and orderly transitions of power. Communal tensions were defused and terrorist leaders arrested. Indonesia did not fragment: a peace deal was reached with the separatist province of Aceh and the search for a solution in equally problematic West Papua initiated.

The result was a decade of economic growth averaging 4.75 per cent per year, and regularly topping 6 per cent by the end of the 2000s. By 2008 the Indonesian economy was twice the size of its pre-crisis peak. The average wealth of Indonesians almost doubled over the same period, and with rising prosperity, domestic consumption increased by nearly 5 per cent each year, making the greater part of the contribution to the growth of the economy. Foreign investment was slow to return and trade continued to play a small role in the newly liberalised economy, but these factors later helped Indonesia sail through the global financial crisis unscathed. A decade after

Suharto's fall there remain reforms that need to be made. Corruption is still rife, and levels of education lag well behind rates of economic development. Observers argue that the momentum for reform has petered out. But Indonesia remains South-East Asia's strongest performer, whose current rates of growth will quickly transform it into a major centre of power.

*

There is a tendency to treat China, Vietnam, India and Indonesia as simply the latest wave of the Asian economic miracle. They are not, either in terms of cause or effect. The Asian 'tigers' of the mid- to late twentieth century all followed a distinct pattern of export-driven growth delivered by protected industries that were nurtured by government intervention. All paid close attention to maintaining compliant, educated workforces, low consumption and high savings, and negligible levels of dissent or tension. The enrichment of none of the Asian tigers – rapid as it was – had a significant effect on the global distribution of wealth and power. Their development altered some of the patterns of production, financing and energy use, but ultimately reinforced the way the world economy functioned.

The rise of the Asian giants is of a different order: in scale and quality, and in cause and effect. The tigers' success was based on discipline and uber-rational planning; none of the giants approaches them in terms of their clarity of vision and their single-minded determination to see it through. Even China – a great admirer of Singapore's achievement, and the great student of Japan's and Korea's methods – has been a hesitant and cautious reformer, willing to roll back what any of the tigers would have seen as crucial reforms in the cause of social order and ideological comfort. The tigers could be rational and disciplined because they were manageable in terms of size and cohesion; the scale of the giants puts these qualities beyond them. The giants' success has nothing to do with the quality or single-mindedness of their reforms. It has everything to do with their size. It's a question of multiplication. Even a moderately positive policy measure will have a major effect if it releases the productivity of hundreds of millions; even a minor gain in productivity will have global effects when multiplied by hundreds of millions. To have an economy larger than Europe's or America's, China or India need to be only one-quarter as productive per person – and they are closing fast.

To the established patterns of world wealth and power, the giants' development has been and will continue to be nothing short of transformative. We are witnessing what Lowy Institute economist Mark Thirlwell has christened 'the great convergence' – the collapse of the centuries-old divide between societies' share of world population and their contribution to global economic activity. The extremes of the great divergence were reached in the mid-1970s, when four-tenths of the world's population produced less than one-tenth of all economic output. Such a lop-sided world will never be seen again. The Asian giants are on their way back to the centrality to the world economy that they enjoyed for the centuries before the West's industrial revolution. Over the next decades, they will reach the stage where they are producing between one-third and one-half of all global economic activity. Their effect on global patterns of consumption, production, finance and energy usage are already profound – and they are still at the beginning of their development process.

The great convergence is also ending the dream run of power and privilege enjoyed by Europe, North America and (riding on their coat-tails) Australasia for two centuries. No longer will a minority of the world's population produce the majority of economic output, or control all of the levers of global power, or be seen as the standard of how to organise a society. They are on their way back to the periphery of the world economy that they occupied for most of history, and their hold on the commanding heights of influence and preference is slipping day by day. The great divide that we thought was inevitable and unbridgeable until so recently is silently vanishing, ushering in a world changed completely.

History's surfers

The twenty years after 1990 – the transmillennial decades – will be looked back on as one of the great pivots of world history. In these years a profound transformation occurred in the world's first, second, fourth and thirteenth most populous societies, with consequences that will shape world order for centuries. It is reasonable to ask why it all happened in these two decades rather than, say, in the 1950s and 1960s when the Asian giants had a clean slate after the end of World War II and the departure of the European colonialists. Or why not later, in the 2020s and 2030s when the effects of population aging and resource exhaustion would have brought Europe's and North America's lead back to more manageable proportions. Looking more closely at the transmillennial years will do more than help us understand the causes of the changes that are happening; it will give us an idea of how long these shifts will continue, and therefore their likely scale and impact.

Let's begin with the starting points of the transformation of each of these giants. The scale and depth of poverty in China, Vietnam, India and Indonesia meant that, once given the chance, they would grow quickly simply because they were starting from a very low base. In 1980, the average wealth per head in China was US$205; in Vietnam it was US$513; in India it was US$263; in Indonesia it was US$644. The only Asian countries with lower per capita wealth than China and India in 1980 were Burma and Nepal. In 1981, 64 per cent of the Chinese population, 60 per cent of Indians, 58 per cent of Vietnamese and 40 per cent of Indonesians lived below the poverty line – US$1.25 per day. Given the chance to escape poverty by modest economic reforms, hundreds of millions of people grasped the chance to improve their fortunes. The ending of agricultural collectivisation and the weakening of restrictions on movement in China and Vietnam, and the unwinding of suffocating licensing frameworks in India and Indonesia, unleashed waves of productive forces into their economies. Even as the aggregate size of the giants' economies surpass those of developed countries, they will remain poor societies. This means that even when their economies are huge, the giants' populations will still contain within them plenty of individual-level energy that will stimulate further strong economic growth.

The rates of poverty in these countries were in large part a consequence of post-independence or post-revolutionary governments that were deeply hostile to capitalism. Those who had fought for independence or revolution were by definition radicals, motivated by the rejection of all they were fighting against and energised by the passion of the fight. They were accustomed to being seen as the fathers of independence or revolution, and were particularly suspicious of alternative sources of power – including those that could emerge internally via the market. The state was their instrument for shaping and controlling the economy and society to their image, interests and vanity. The countries they benchmarked against were the products of the age of heavy industry and mass production, and so the nations that these new leaders wanted to build had to compete in the high-prestige sectors of heavy industry, chemicals and nuclear technology. Invariably the preference of post-independence and post-revolutionary leaders was for some combination of a range of familiar policy instruments: nationalisation of industry, collectivisation of agriculture, import substitution, rigid control if not eradication of private economic activity, and a deep aversion to foreign investment, currency convertability and the cross-border flow of capital. In some cases, industries that were internationally competitive at independence, such as India's textile sector, were weighed down with requirements designed to boost employment levels. At times, the economy was seen as an extension of the independence struggle or the revolution, and disastrous experiments such as the Great Leap Forward were insufficient to deter the repeat of similar attempts.

This post-independence and post-revolutionary experience eventually gave rise to a deep conviction in these societies that the combination of charismatic leadership, state-directed development, and economic autarchy had failed. There was a deep weariness with state planning and sudden exhortations for greater collective efforts to develop the country. For all of the resistance to liberalising reforms among privileged elites, there was a great receptivity to new policies that removed power and incentives from the hands of bureaucrats and regulators. With the passing of Mao Zedong, Le Duan, the Gandhi dynasty and Suharto – and the generations they led – the reformist leaders of the giants were able to quietly move away from those independence-era policies. The reformers were aware of what the Asian tigers had achieved, indeed those in China and Vietnam were heartened that economies could be liberalised while preserving for the state a good measure of political and social control. The support of the masses often came after the fact, in the form of stunning growth rates and booming productivity. The reformers invested faith in the people over the state as the force of innovation and growth in the economy, and the people responded with spectacular results.

The giants were not only poor, they were huge and densely populated. This meant they had vast reserves of very cheap labour, and China and India had domestic markets larger than any possible comparator. They offered international companies scale economies that had dazzled business brains for centuries. The size of their markets and abundance of cheap and productive labour meant that the giants could grow rapidly despite a very average performance in terms of reforms and governance. The size of the giants also means that they can afford to be less concerned about the effects on international investment of corruption, crumbling infrastructure and slothful bureaucracies. India's poor governance, bad infrastructure and high corruption are estimated to wipe nearly 2 percentage points off its annual economic growth rate – and still it grows at 8.5 per cent a year. The World Bank estimates that governance failures suppress foreign direct investment to China by 30 per cent – yet it remains the world's largest destination for such funds.

The size of the giants has also given their governments greater latitude to experiment with reforms through trial and error and learning by doing, without risking the performance of the whole economy. Part of the reason their reform progress has appeared so piecemeal and spasmodic has been that they have had the luxury of being able to experiment, pause, evaluate and innovate. And the giants' size advantages only increase as they continue to grow. Few international companies can long deflect shareholders' questions about why they are not yet producing or doing business in China. Few businesses are unaware of the breathless calculations being made about the projected size of the Chinese and Indian middle classes.

A big part of the 'perfect storm' for the giants was the acceleration of globalisation that occurred in the 1980s, 1990s and beyond. The late twentieth-century surge of globalisation itself had several drivers. One was the arrival of lower growth rates and a more liberal cast of mind in the West, which had led to a remarkable opening up of the developed world to interactions with the developing world. Immigration restrictions were relaxed and the international education sector was promoted, leading to a sudden and rapid increase in people from the developing world residing in developed countries.

The advent of cheaper and more seamless international travel increased the interaction across the development gap even further. Another driver of globalisation was the sudden build up of internationally mobile finance, initially driven by the accumulation of petrodollars after the 1970s oil shocks. The rapid growth in financial transactions increased pressure on the developed world to float exchange rates, liberalise financial sectors and facilitate international investment. The growth in trade volumes outstripped world economic growth as trade and investment barriers were progressively dismantled in the West.

The birth and acceleration of the information and communications technology (ICT) revolution has been the most powerful driver of globalisation. The ICT revolution has gone far beyond what used to be called 'the digital divide': internet use has increased 16-fold in China, ten-fold in India and nine-fold in Indonesia over the past decade. Mobile phone use has increased seven-fold in China, 86-fold in India and 34-fold in Indonesia over the same period. The ICT revolution has facilitated the internationalisation of production, allowing companies to locate different sections of their manufacturing chains in countries offering the cheapest and most productive workforce, access to cheap energy and appropriate resources, and friendliest investment climate. It has powered the growth and internationalisation of the global services sector, now the most dynamic sector in the global economy. It has accelerated cycles of innovation, knowledge transfer and technology adoption, thus powering an increasingly international knowledge-intensive economy. It has expanded networks and possibilities for innovation, favouring newer, smaller, hungrier businesses in many sectors of the economy. And perhaps most importantly, the ICT revolution has spread an awareness of the privileges of the West among developing countries. Nothing has been so corrosive to the fatalism and acceptance of their lot in life of people in poor, remote rural communities than the arrival of the internet, mobile phones and cable television. Nothing has so eroded the belief that differences in people's situations derive from in-born traits. Nothing has so detonated the burst of entrepreneurial energy in the developing world as the knowledge of how the other half lives – and the ability to access the means to get there.

A vital connection between the giants and the world economy has been their diasporas. Three of the world's great diasporas originate in Asia: the Chinese, the Indian and the Muslim. Chinese, Indians and Muslims have been fanning out from their homelands for centuries, settling in other societies and often becoming the centres of entrepreneurialism and finance in their newly adopted societies. Just as often, they faced suspicion and even persecution from their host societies. Often the largest, most crowded and poorest societies produce the strongest outflows; and consequently the Chinese (over 33 million) and Indians (over 25 million) are the two largest diasporas on the planet. Particularly the overseas Chinese played a vital role in channelling investment back into a liberalising Chinese economy. They also provided trusted linkages into export markets. It was members of the diasporas who best understood conditions, sensitivities and possibilities in the awakening giants, and who often led the international investment surge into China and India. It was ethnic-based networks that first established fast, flexible production chains between low-cost workforces in Asia and rapidly evolving markets in the West.

Overseas Chinese – and later mainlanders – and Indians were among the most eager to take advantage of the liberalisation of immigration and educations systems in the West. Many went to North America, Europe and Australasia to study engineering and finance. A study by California's Public Policy Institute showed that 60 per cent of all foreign-born software engineers in Silicon Valley by the 1990s were either Chinese or Indian immigrants, and that Chinese and Indian diasporas were active in establishing ethnic professional associations which in turn drew even more of their ethnic kin into hi-tech sectors of the economy. Often a perception of being blocked from management positions led to a high raté of founding new companies by Chinese and Indian IT professionals, who equally often drew on ethnic networks for investment and to build initial business. Ultimately these Western-educated diasporas provided the vital linkages and knowledge to those who returned to China or India to start up their own companies there, and make the most of low-cost but educated workforces. Diasporas became the basis of transnational networks of trust and familiarity that were particularly well suited to compete in rapidly evolving industries with very tight production cycles of months rather than years.

*

While the transmillennial years were good to Australia, making it wealthier, more productive and more globally engaged than ever before, they also saw an epochal change in the societies to its north. Remarkably, the rise of the teeming billions to Australia's north occurred at the time when mainstream Australia had stopped fearing that eventuality. After nearly two centuries of fearing the 'yellow peril', there are few Western societies that regard a wealthy and powerful China with more optimism and less dread than Australians. A large part of the reason is that the rise of the giants – like the rise of the tigers before them – has been an unadulterated good news story for Australia. Few Australians are now unaware that Chinese demand for Australian resources has boosted its economic performance over the past decade and has helped it, alone out of the countries of the West, escape the global financial crisis.

But fear and optimism are too narrow a range of lenses for viewing the magnitude of the change that is happening. The growing wealth of these huge societies is already conferring power and influence on their governments – and this is occurring in an era when power and influence are manifested in very different ways than we are used to historically. The next chapters will examine what the giants' power and influence look like, and how they are likely to wield – or not wield – these attributes.

The geometry
of power

3

I t may offend our egalitarian sensibilities, but societies need power
to function. There can be no society without power, and a society
without powerful people would be compelled to invent them. Power
establishes patterns and signposts determining what can be done and
what can't. To live our lives, we need to know who's in charge, who's
responsible, who it's wise not to cross, who makes things happen.
We pay close attention to powerful people because their actions set
the eddies and currents that shape our daily lives. They are powerful

because of the position they occupy or the resources they command. Their decisions have a greater impact on society than those of ordinary people. Their opinions command attention. Their tastes and actions fascinate, inspire or outrage people whom they have never heard of, and never will. A powerful person is able to call on a much greater range of connections, resources and authority than an ordinary person. Their capacity to influence their surroundings is much greater than their surroundings' ability to influence them.

Power is just as important to how the world works. Powerful countries can shape the rhythms and tides of international affairs when they want to – and sometimes when they don't. They are threatened by few, but they can inspire either fear or reassurance in many. Their companies create and satisfy the planet's appetites, their bourses send shudders or surges through global markets, their currencies signal the ebbs and flows of world economic fortunes. Other societies know much more about their social mores and preferences, elections and geographies than powerful countries' citizens know about the outside world. Their scientists and engineers are able to achieve things that are beyond the capacities and imaginations of their colleagues in smaller countries. Powerful countries are often identified with the hopes or antipathies of people who live elsewhere and may never have visited them. Their presence or absence determines whether an international meeting should be taken seriously. Their preferences and choices carry great weight, and when they agree among each other, their decisions can apply to all humanity. When they disagree, planetary action stalls.

But power works much more informally among countries than within them. Formal positions do not determine who is powerful in international affairs. Some positions look impressive – a permanent seat on the United Nations Security Council for example – but these can be occupied by countries that are no longer powerful. Nor do powerful countries have established schedules of duties and prerogatives that come with their position. They have an almost limitless menu of roles they can choose to play, or not play, on the world stage. And there is no formal division of capacities and responsibilities among the great powers. They tend to try to be strong and influential across all capabilities at the same time, but more often than not they fail. There is no set number or range of powerful countries in international affairs: there can be half a dozen at one time, or there can be one.

What is most confusing is that there is no event, ceremony or threshold that establishes a country's great power status unambiguously. Lists of great powers are subjective, and evidence of a power's eclipse is often as convincing as evidence for its continued rise. Sometimes a country is not accorded great power status until well after it has the requisite strength, and just as often it continues to hold that status long after its strength justifies it. Great powers themselves have more than a little at stake in trying to determine who stays out and who comes into the great power club. The ultimate test of the hierarchy of international power is a direct test of wills – an event which itself can radically change the great power order, not to mention ending all life on earth.

For all its importance to how the world works, the global power equation is never stable. Constantly fluctuating cycles of wealth, demography, technology, and political fission and fusion reshuffle the international deck incessantly. The long list of once-great powers that are now just tourist attractions ought to be a cautionary tale about the inevitable transience of power. And yet it isn't. There is not one great power that has existed free of the belief that its position atop the global hierarchy reflects deep, innate, timeless qualities within its society. What's more, it is often the obligations undertaken as part of a great power's self-belief that can most quickly erode its strength, while its confidence in its innate qualities blinds it to the hollowing out of its power.

All of this means that working out the global power diagram is a highly subjective art form. There are those who try to make it scientific, by converting it all to numbers: of missiles and soldiers, of foreign reserves and economic size, of population and position. Two Chinese professors have for some years been measuring 'comprehensive national power' by totting up countries' proportions of the world's stock of certain 'strategic resources'. But ultimately the results of these studies bear little relation to what happens in the real world. Superpowers collapse, or are defeated by small insurgencies, or both. Tottering dictatorships can hold the world to ransom. Great powers, whose decline has been confidently predicted, can suddenly surge back to a position of unrivalled strength. In the end, the things you choose to count, and how you put them all into the same big equation, depends on preferences and biases you may not even realise you hold.

But for all of this uncertainty, there is no more important question than the status and ordering of global power. This is about much more than just bragging rights. Great powers command such forces of production, and destruction, that their choices ultimately shape what other societies are able to do. In no other field of human affairs is the fate of so many held in the hands of so few. So countries and corporations, movements and media, need to know which countries matter, how they matter and when they matter as they plan and operate globally. Sudden shifts in the global pecking order can change the operating conditions for a broad range of international activities. To understand how any crisis, stand-off or development will play out, we first need to ask which powerful countries are interested, what their preferences are, and how much leverage they have compared to other interested powerful countries.

To make it even harder, it is not just a matter of which countries are powerful at any given point in time. This question alone generates such contention and debate that it is usually the only question that is asked. To one particularly abstract way of thinking about these issues, simply knowing how many great powers there are in the world can tell you a whole lot more about how the world works. But simply trying to establish how many great powers there are is pointless without thinking hard about a prior question: how power works in international affairs, and how it is changing. Most people who think a great deal about these things tend to assume that international power is a single currency that has changed very little over the centuries. And there are quite a few who seem to assume that there is a finite stock of power in the world – much like energy in a closed system – that is shared among its constituent units. The more one player has, the less there is to be distributed among the rest; as one player's stock grows, it ebbs away from others. But to see world power in so mechanistic a way makes little sense when so much is changing in international affairs. How can power in the early twenty-first century work in basically the same ways as it worked in the early twentieth, when the past hundred years has seen the appearance of nuclear weapons and the internet, the disappearance of empires and warring monarchs, and the advent of a genuinely global system of international affairs that is increasingly monitored and co-ordinated through satellites orbiting far from the globe's surface?

Power in the twenty-first century has changed – in the way it works, how it is distributed, and what it can do – from how it has worked for most of human history. What has changed it is connectedness, or the multiple strands that link up human activities across borders and great distances, in a way that can cause seemingly small decisions to have major consequences a long way away. This means that power is harder to see and measure, and it is much harder to use for clear ends with predictable consequences. Different countries are becoming powerful in different ways, and their different power holdings contradict, reinforce or transform each other in diverse ways. And it is not only countries that have significant power in the twenty-first century. The causes that most passionately motivate people in our world are not identified with nations but with transnational movements, and can seriously complicate the agendas of national governments and international agencies. The result of all of this global evolution has been to usher in what former Canadian diplomat Daryl Copeland calls a 'heteropolar world' – a complex, messy dynamic of international affairs which blends different forms of power, different agendas, and different types of actor in unpredictable and constantly evolving ways. It is on this stage that the great convergence is unfolding, and as the Asian giants rise they are playing into the variable geometry of power that shapes world affairs. We need to understand how power works before we can begin to judge how the great convergence will affect the global ladder of influence.

Command and consequence

In June 1995, a tall distinguished-looking gentleman of Chinese background attended an anniversary function at Cornell University. Like many of the other international alumni, he had arrived in the United States with a tourist visa before making his way to his alma mater. He obviously enjoyed the celebrations, catching up with former colleagues and friends and wandering through familiar buildings. But there was more media interest in this gentleman than there was in any of the other alumni, or than there had been in past visits by some of Cornell's most distinguished alumni.

He was the president of Taiwan, Lee Teng-hui, and his visit to the United States had caused the most serious international crisis since the fall of the Berlin Wall. China had become increasingly irritated by what it viewed as Lee's subtle campaign to emphasise Taiwan's independence from China. Beijing's highest priority has always been to isolate Taiwan by excluding it from international agencies and persuading other countries not to accord it full diplomatic recognition. In a decades-long global public relations battle, Taiwan has pursued any and all symbols of its independent status it can get, while China has sought to deny it any acknowledgement that it is anything but a renegade province. To a leadership in Beijing keen to demonstrate their hard-nosed credentials in the context of their own recent transfer of power, Lee's visit to the United States crossed a red line. He might have gone on a tourist visa, but it was the self-styled president of a renegade province making a statesman-like visit to the country that underwrote its independence bid.

Amid a storm of angry rhetoric that followed, China announced a series of missile tests and live-fire military exercises in the Taiwan Straits. In July and August, missiles were fired from the Chinese coastline, hitting the ocean within 200 kilometres of Taiwan's capital and its major trading port in the north. Despite international calls for calm, Beijing turned its anger towards Lee's bid for re-election in March 1996. In November, a Chinese Foreign Ministry spokesman warned that Beijing regarded the election as part of Lee's strategy to promote the image of Taiwan as an independent country. In early January, a senior official announced that Beijing would consider all measures 'to expose and stop Lee Teng-hui's plot of breaking up the motherland and pursuing independence for Taiwan'. Once again, military exercises were staged on sections of the Chinese coastline topographically similar to Taiwan's coasts. Plans for further missile launches were publicised. As the election countdown began, four unarmed missiles were fired into the sea just 40 kilometres from Taiwan's two major harbours, through which 70 per cent of its trade passed. The Taiwanese stock exchange lost one-third of its value over the space of a fortnight, and foreign exchange reserves dropped by a fifth.

But as an exercise in power and intimidation, the missile tests and military exercises failed. Lee was re-elected in a landslide, winning 54 per cent of the popular vote. China's belligerence so angered many Taiwanese that in the next presidential poll they elected a hard-line pro-independence candidate. The crisis succeeded in emphasising to the world media Taiwan's transition to a fully fledged democracy just seven years after pro-democracy protests had been brutally crushed in China. Taiwan attracted a wave of international sympathy and admiration for its courage many times greater than years of persistent diplomacy and aid payments had managed to elicit. The island's vigorous democracy underlined its insistence that it would only unify with China with the full consent of its people.

The show of force around Taiwan damaged China's international interests. The missile tests prompted the United States to send two aircraft carrier battle groups into the Taiwan Straits – a demonstration of just how much more militarily potent America was than its closest rival. Support for Taiwan hardened in the United States Congress, ensuring regular weapons sales to the island and significant opposition to Beijing's bid to join the World Trade Organisation in subsequent years. Beijing's belligerence also set back its patient campaign to normalise its image and international relationships after the public relations disaster of the Tiananmen massacre of June 1989. Isolated by Western countries after that crackdown, China had relied on its Asian neighbours for its earliest acceptance back into polite international society. Japan was the first major country to reach out after Tiananmen, announcing a major development loan package to China in 1990 and publicly sympathising with Beijing's defence of its human rights standards. But the Taiwan Straits crisis prompted concern in Japan about China's rising power. The following month Tokyo significantly strengthened its defence alliance with the United States, and in the ensuing years gradually ceased development assistance to China. Several other South-East Asian states were also alarmed by China's militaristic approach to the crisis, an impression deepened by the Philippines' clashes with the Chinese navy in the South China Sea the following year. Worst of all, the fallout from the crisis gave Taiwan the space to further push the limits. Over the next few years Taipei was able to make small but symbolic assertions of its independence secure in the knowledge that Beijing could not object forcefully without further damaging years of patient bridge-building diplomacy in the region. Taiwan has had three presidential elections since 1996, two of which have elected the hard-line pro-independence candidate Chen Shui-bian. In all three, China has kept its missiles quietly in their silos.

The most direct way to get someone to do what you want is to force them to do it. Almost as direct, but often more expensive, is to bribe them to do it. The power to command through coercion or inducement is the most basic form of power within and among societies, and has been the leverage of first choice for countries through most of history. Modern states evolved into their present form by constantly striving to find the best ways to build the capacity to inflict damage on others and to amass great financial resources. Just as they did 500 years ago, countries today build their military and financial strength with one eye on the possibility that they may want to command certain international outcomes, and the other eye on being able to dissuade other countries from trying to demand their own compliance. The power to command and the power to thwart others' demands are functions of the capacity to inflict damage or buy compliance.

There are two different types of 'command power' in world affairs. The most direct and intense type is constant control over another country across a broad range of its interests and choices. This is the type of relationship that the Soviet Union established over Poland, Hungary and the other Warsaw Pact countries after World War II. It allowed Moscow a great measure of control over these smaller countries' political systems, foreign policy choices, trading relationships, industrial and technology investments and, from time to time, the way they handled internal dissent. Ultimately maintaining such a control relationship was hugely resource-intensive for the Soviet Union, even though it was so much larger than its subject countries. The need for tight control meant constant, close monitoring of these countries' political and social dynamics, and maintaining the ever-present threat of coercive force or economic strangulation. But the greatest cost was to the legitimacy of the Soviet Union's relationships with these countries of Eastern and Central Europe. The longer the control lasted, and the more often the use or threat of coercion was made, the greater were the pressures to dissolve the unequal partnerships. As soon as Soviet President Mikhail Gorbachev showed the slightest unwillingness to resort to coercive force to restore order in Eastern Europe in the autumn of 1989, Moscow's 'alliances' in the region unravelled overnight. Member after erstwhile member of the Warsaw Pact wasted little opportunity in joining the opposing NATO alliance in the 1990s, primarily as a way of putting the greatest possible distance between themselves and the prospect of a resurgence of Moscow's controlling relationship.

A much more common form of control is the ability to achieve the country's objectives by shaping the choices and behaviour of other countries through threats or inducements. It was this type of control that American President James Monroe had in mind when he rose to present his seventh State of the Union speech to Congress in December 1823. Responding to the intention of the Russian, Austrian and Prussian Emperors to try to re-establish the rule of the House of Bourbon over Spain's disintegrating empire in the Americas, Monroe proclaimed that 'the American continents, by the free and independent condition which they have assumed and maintain, are henceforth not to be considered as subjects for future colonization by any European powers'. Though president of a nation of just 11 million, Monroe made clear that his proclamation would be backed by force: 'we should consider any attempt on their part to extend [European domination] to any portion of this hemisphere, as dangerous to our peace and safety ... as the manifestation of an unfriendly disposition towards the United States'. Unlike the Soviet Union's relationships with its Warsaw Pact allies, the United States was not proposing to try to control all aspects of Russian, Austrian or Prussian behaviour. It was seeking only to influence the three emperors' choices about whether or not to intervene in the Americas by signalling that any such attempt would be met by American force. That the Monroe Doctrine was an effective display of power is proven by its one failure – France's invasion of Mexico in 1863, when the United States was unable to resist due to its own civil war. For the rest of the passage of time since Monroe's speech European powers have judged it too potentially costly, for little prospective gain, to try to set foot in the Americas.

This is the base currency of international affairs: an ever-recalibrating series of calculations about what can be gained by threat, force or inducement – and at what cost. The constant recalibration of these equations occurs at a micro-level and at a macro-level. Micro-level recalibrations happen between countries and groups of countries that constantly watch each other's levels of wealth and might, and constantly do the maths around what they could achieve by threat, force or inducement and at what cost. Macro-level recalibrations occur just as regularly, and along two axes. The first is that states continue to get better and better at devising ways to cause each other damage: each generation of weapons systems is more potent than the last. The second axis is that states continue to get better and better at amassing wealth. They have abandoned old beliefs that the way to wealth lies in becoming industrially self-reliant and distorting trade to allow the country to pile up gold bullion, and realised that wealth is created much faster by dismantling barriers to trade, finance and the internationalisation of production. The result is a strange mix: a world in which countries have never been as dependent on each other for their wealth and their basic capacity to function, while being able to do each other greater damage than ever before. The potential gains from outright coercion have become much less obvious (with an increasingly open world economy, what's to be gained by force?) while the potential costs continue to rise. Not only is the decision to threaten or use force more consequential and unpredictable as the potency of weapons rises, but the potential for force to disrupt the flows of global commerce continues to mount. It's easy to start a war; it's impossible to predict how it will end or what it will destroy. Little wonder that the incidence of conflict among states has fallen to all-time historic lows.

What's more, it is getting harder and harder to justify using or threatening coercion, or blatantly buying compliance. Each decision by a country to go to war is increasingly choked by legal advice, lengthy justifications and counter-arguments, and forensic post-mortems and inquiries. The ever-contracting ambit of legitimate reasons for threatening or using coercion continually raises the political costs of using force. It also means that the likelihood that force will be resisted is rising all the time, and that any gains from coercion, threat or inducement will be strongly contested far into the future. But for all the fading utility of command power, countries still invest vastly more in weapons than in diplomats. This should not be taken as a sign that they're gearing up for war. What they're doing is making war less likely by increasing the potential costs to those that choose to revert to coercion. The correlations of violence have not vanished from world affairs but they have moved to the background. Numbers and dispositions of nuclear weapons, aircraft carriers and missiles, stealth fighters and submarines form the basic skeleton of world affairs. They're not the main drivers of action but they're the main determinants of what can be done and what can't.

Other forms of power have stepped in to form the muscles and imagination of world affairs, taking over roles that command power has played for most of human history.

Gravity bites

As societies and economies intertwine and enrich each other, a different form of power is becoming increasingly important to how the world works. This is the gravitational effect that large and rapidly changing economies can have on the fortunes and choices of other societies. The tidal effects of the growth rates of the Asian giants reach further, faster and deeper in an increasingly globalised world. Emerging economies – particularly very large ones – are almost always more volatile than established ones, making their fortunes much more central to the fortunes of the global economy than their absolute economic size would suggest. Their scale and rate of change within an increasingly seamless global economy enables, displaces and reshapes economic activity and its social and political consequences far beyond Asia. For example, at their current rates of population growth, China and India are adding over 40 million workers to the global economy annually – the equivalent of the arrival of another France in the world economy every year. This has relentlessly undercut employment rates and wage growth in the rest of the global economy, hitting first and hardest in those parts of the world with the highest-paid workers. The result has been high and growing structural unemployment, growing inequality, burgeoning pressure on the welfare state, and deepening intergenerational and political conflict within societies whose aging and shrinking populations would otherwise have eased the employment creation pressures on sluggish economies. But the tides have not been all negative. China and India have driven down prices of manufactured products and services around the world, contributing in a major way to the very low rates of inflation in most countries during the transmillennial decades, while China's surplus in savings financed the consumption boom in the developed world.

Gravitational influence is very different to the direct power to command, because its effects are often completely unintended by the giant that has caused them. This becomes particularly obvious when we see the extent to which China's and India's demand for energy and resources has shifted the terms of trade sharply against their own economic interests. The scale and growth of the giants' resources and energy thirst has led to a sudden sharp rise in the prices of the commodities they need to import, even while they hold down prices of the products they sell to the rest of the world.

Another unintended effect has been on the perceptions and expectations of people in other societies about the responsibilities of the giants. China's and India's impact on global challenges such as climate change has markedly increased awareness around the world of how central they are to any solution, and a growing expectation that they will shoulder global obligations commensurate with their gravitational impact. This is profoundly uncomfortable for Beijing and New Delhi, which see themselves very much as developing countries with no historical responsibility for such problems. But the size and rate of growth of the giants will make it very hard to prevail with such an argument indefinitely.

Yet while gravitational influence cannot be deployed with precision to reach defined objectives, it can be leveraged. China's vast, cheap and disciplined workforce, and the country's economic openness (the value of its trade is almost three-quarters as large as its entire economy), has made it increasingly central to international production chains and trade flows. Of the 21 members of APEC, China is the largest trading partner of six; second- or third-largest for another five; and in the top five trading partners of four more. This makes Beijing's choices globally important well beyond global manufacturing. For example, amid the growing controversy over the valuation of national currencies, China's choices on its renminbi will determine the choices of at least half a dozen other manufacturing economies in Asia which have their currencies pegged to the US dollar but their economic fortunes overwhelmingly determined by their trading competitiveness with China. China's growing centrality to the economic fortunes of so many countries is useful for Beijing in yet another way. With each passing month, more countries acquire a greater stake in China's economic dynamism and success. There could have been no greater reassurance against Beijing's fears of containment and isolation than when most of the world caught its breath in mid-2007 as the Shanghai stock exchange plunged overnight.

Another gravitational benefit that accrues to large and dynamic societies is deference and admiration. Nothing inspires like success. The rate and consistency of China's growth over three decades has engendered admiration, particularly among populations in the developing world. South-East Asian societies which between the 1940s and the 1990s suppressed their Chinese minorities – banning their ceremonies, language and calligraphy, suppressing their business activities, and forcing them to adopt non-Chinese names – suddenly began allowing, if not celebrating, the open expression of Chinese-ness. Chinese minorities that were once seen as unscrupulous shysters or dangerous subversives suddenly became the symbols of economic vitality and of the connections between the local economy and a booming China. China, and latterly India, have replaced Japan as the talisman of Asian success on their own terms, without depending on Western advice and largesse. And the prominence of their example has been illuminated by the sudden collapse and lingering malaise of the North Atlantic economies after late 2007.

Little leaders

When Singapore became an independent country on 9 August 1965, few thought it would last long. For centuries it had been a pawn in the great chessboard of competition between Siamese, Malay, Portuguese, Dutch and British empires. Leading a new country that was plagued by housing shortages, high unemployment, ethnic and labour unrest, and disease in its mushrooming squatter settlements, Singapore's prime minister wept as he announced independence. With no natural resources and surging population growth, it was dependent on Malaysia for its water supplies and Indonesian goodwill for the shipping that passed through its port. Singapore's 1.9 million people, 70 per cent of whom were ethnic Chinese, were surrounded by an archipelago of resentful Malays: Malaysia's 10 million and Indonesia's 106 million. The Parliament of Malaysia had voted unanimously to expel Singapore from the federation, but there were also powerful voices in Kuala Lumpur calling for its forceful re-incorporation on draconian terms. Jakarta claimed Singapore as part of Indonesia Raya (Greater Indonesia) and waged a campaign of aggression and sedition under its Konfrontasi (Confrontation) strategy. Soon after independence, Britain announced it would be withdrawing its troops from Singapore.

Singapore not only survived, within a generation it had become the most influential diplomatic actor in its region. The key to its remarkable success was its co-founding of the Association of South-East Asian Nations (ASEAN) just one day short of the second anniversary of its independence. Originally designed as a way of calming frictions between Indonesia, Malaysia and the Philippines, ASEAN's five countries (those three plus Singapore and Thailand) soon established a strong sense of solidarity in a region buffeted by the ripples from the wars in Vietnam and Cambodia and the Cultural Revolution in China. By the late 1990s, when it had expanded to include all ten South-East Asian countries, ASEAN was regarded as the most successful regional organisation outside Europe, and its regular leaders' summits commanded audiences with the leaders of all of the major countries involved in the region. Singapore's diplomats and intellectuals emerged as important and provocative voices for Asian solidarity and influence beyond the region. When other ASEAN countries reacted defensively to proposals for broader regional groupings, such as APEC, Singapore saw an opportunity. It argued quietly that these proposals should be supported – but on the condition that ASEAN be placed firmly at the centre of any new regional initiative. And so APEC came into being having formally enshrined ASEAN's principles of consensus-only action, and on the agreement that every second meeting be held in South-East Asia. The APEC Secretariat was established in 1992 – in Singapore. The ASEAN centrality principle was born, and incorporated in every regional body that followed. When powerful countries wanted to back one proposal or another, Singapore was one of the first places they courted. But when Singapore objected to a proposal, such as Australian Prime Minister Kevin Rudd's initiative to form an Asia Pacific Community, it could mobilise a blocking ASEAN coalition against it.

City-states have been powerful throughout history, but they have relied on conventional means – force and money – to wield influence. Singapore prospered because the world into which it was born was uniquely designed to reward clever, persistent diplomacy, irrespective of the size or location of the country practising it. From the middle of the twentieth century, nations began founding and working through international organisations at a rate never seen before. At the beginning of the twentieth century there were just 37 international agencies, co-ordinating fairly mundane services like international postage and global telegraph traffic. By the end of the century there were 50 times as many, uniting regions or spanning the globe, addressing issues of war and peace, disease and poverty, energy and finance. The real spurt in constructing international co-operation occurred in the early 1980s, with the number of intergovernmental agencies increasing five-fold between 1978 and 1985.

The effect of this on the way the world works has been nothing short of transformative. Governments have completely reshaped their diplomatic instruments and agendas around their growing numbers of intergovernmental commitments. The agenda of international meetings now shapes the travel schedules and work rhythms of the leaders of most countries on earth. Even more profound has been the remoulding of governments' international expectations and aspirations. With the growing number of international meetings has come a growing awareness of collective challenges. And with the growing awareness of collective challenges has come a growing realisation of the dynamic linkages between challenges and issues – climate change and disease; the internet and crime; pension reform and financial volatility. All of this has led to a propensity to consult, if not always to collaborate, among governments, and to an expectation that nearly every international action and reaction will involve some form of negotiation or discussion in an intergovernmental agency. But the expanding domain of international co-operation has not brought us to a nirvana of global peace, justice and goodwill; states are just as venal, competitive and duplicitous within international agencies as they are outside.

International organisations, if used cleverly, can be powerful amplifiers of individual countries' influence. Their memberships, rules and agendas can be shaped to direct attention to some issues and obscure others. They can enshrine clear hierarchies of power, leadership and control that are near impossible to change against the will of those they favour. They can be used to 'seize' issues – and thereby make it hard for other groupings to attend them – and determine the shape and pace or lack of progress towards possible solutions. They can be mobilised into blocs that can deliver either success or failure to a broader initiative. They can be used to stop members from saying or doing what they would like to, or to shape the behaviour of non-members that want to join.

The international propensity to consult and co-ordinate bends and warps the workings of power among countries. Some, by occupying certain positions or through diplomatic craft, can exercise influence well beyond what their size and significance would suggest. International agencies allow countries with the will to lead and build coalitions a powerful platform from which to shape the flow of international events. They are usually skilful in concealing their own objectives behind appeals to the greater good, and clever in mobilising enough countries of sufficient consequence behind their own definition of the problem and the solution. Contrary to what one would expect, big countries that are powerful in conventional ways usually find international meetings uncomfortable. They are expected to lead, but scrutinised doubly for any hint of self-interest in their proposals. They face the constant fear that their initiatives will fall flat or provoke a storm of opposition. Few countries will mobilise to help the powerful negotiate a solution or build support, but the entire organisation will eagerly monitor whether a major country is faithful to the solution it has advocated. When they oppose a mooted collective action, they are universally blamed for the organisation's failure to act. And so with the big players unusually passive, international agencies often become the arenas for nimble and clever diplomacy by small and mid-sized countries.

*

This then is the structure of the heteropolar world in which we live. Three types of power and influence shape this world: command, gravity, and social activism. Different countries possess different amounts of each. The old behemoths – America, Europe, Russia, and Japan – still possess the most command power. They are able to muster more capacity to hurt or money to influence than the vast majority of other countries, and for that reason alone, they are listened to and followed. But their current economic atrophy, demographic crises and internal political malaise means they have little gravitational power; neither their sluggish growth nor their periodic crises cause more than a ripple in other parts of the world. And their long history of controlling world affairs encourages suspicions that seriously handicap their capacity to leverage their influence through international organisations.

The new behemoths – China, India, Indonesia and perhaps Vietnam and Brazil – are awakening to the attention and admiration that comes from being big and dynamic. But beyond the occasional leveraging of this status, none have worked out how to use this prominence to get what they want. They have found that their ability to command and buy direct outcomes is a blunt and unpredictable instrument, which paradoxically is seen as less potent than it is, but one that still frightens the neighbourhood when it is unsheathed. Their size and prominence makes them awkward players in international negotiations, all too aware of the risks of attempting to lead, but occasionally exhilarated by their capacity to block significant international action on such issues as trade or climate change.

In between the old and the new behemoths are the mid-sized movers and shakers, countries well aware of what they have to lose in a world dominated by the forces of command and gravity, but also alive to the creative possibilities to buttress their own agendas amidst those fluid and varied power dynamics. Within such a fluctuating and lop-sided set of capacities and liabilities, it is impossible to assemble a definitive power table. Great powers no longer all look alike.

Power's highways

The contending, colluding spheres of power in our world do not shape all parts of the Earth's surface in recurring patterns and shades. Most parts of the Earth are left largely untouched, to shape their own dynamics according to the preferences and prejudices of the countries that are etched on them. On the other hand, the courses along which the great powers interact become deeply scoured and elaborately shaped with the patterns and consequences of the constant traffic of rivalry and enrichment. These are power's highways. Few countries that lie along power's highways can avoid being shaped by the traffic. The clever are enriched; the unlucky and unprepared are ruined.

At least half of the actions of powerful countries are motivated by their perceived vulnerabilities, and the rest by what they think they can achieve. Often the opportunities and the risks lie along the same courses, because big, dynamic societies are each others' greatest dangers and greatest prospects at one and the same time. The broad plains of central Asia linked imperial China, medieval Europe and the Muslim empires, for centuries enriching and imperilling each. The folkways and trade lanes of the Mediterranean and maritime South-East Asia were the pathways of exchange, conversion and conquest for thousands of years. The shipping routes across the Atlantic underpinned the surges in wealth and technology and revolutions in thought and ideology that brought us to the modern world. The intensity of the North Atlantic traffic also brought the destruction of the two greatest wars ever seen, followed by an astonishing post-modern experiment of conciliation, cohabitation and mutual enrichment that is the European Union. So repeatedly did power course backwards and forth across the North Atlantic that the older highways – across the heart of Asia and around its southern and eastern coastlines – fell gradually into disuse.

But even as the traffic reached its peak across the Atlantic in the twentieth century, a new path of contention and reaction began to be sketched across the Pacific Ocean. It was here that for the first time in centuries a major European power was beaten in a war by a non-European country. By mid-century, the rivalry between the first modern Asian power and the established North Atlantic powers had turned into a war of conquest and reconquest, made all the more brutal by contending civilisational prerogatives. The war stopped but the fighting didn't. A virulent form of communism sprouted and spread, made more dangerous and aggressive as it cross-bred with bitter righteousness of anti-colonial nationalism. The virus captured Asia's largest country and began to infect the others. It provoked the Cold War's two bloodiest conflicts, in Korea and Vietnam, and kept two others smouldering, in the Taiwan Straits and Cambodia.

The best form of inoculation that the victorious World War II allies could think of for China's neighbours was stability and development. Across the new Pacific power highway they built a system of alliances, stretching from San Francisco to Tokyo, Seoul, Taipei, Manila, Bangkok, and Canberra and Wellington. Investment and trade began to course backwards and forwards on the highway, alongside troops, arms and aircraft carriers. As early as the 1960s a dynamic cycle of enrichment and assurance had begun to trace the coastlines of the Pacific Ocean. It linked societies that complemented each other neatly: the world's wealthiest consumers in North America; resource-poor, crowded, disciplined and industrious North-East Asia; the abundant cheap labour of South-East Asia; and Australia's full-spectrum abundance of high-quality energy and minerals. The result was the most astonishing enrichment the world had ever seen, with the non-communist societies along Asia's eastern coast its beneficiaries.

This new power highway was given a name: the Asia Pacific. It joined the world's two largest economies and its first, third and fourth largest countries. Tended by the largest overseas commit-ments of American forces outside of Europe, the Asia Pacific power highway joined the North Atlantic power highway as the twin pivots of world affairs. In the process of their transformation, the societies of the western Pacific were effectively detached from the rest of the Asian continent. Their links with the societies on the other side of the Pacific Ocean were more immediate, dynamic and essential than their relations with the countries to their immediate west. And as they joined the world-wide trend towards establishing regional organisations in the 1990s, they followed these patterns. Asia Pacific regionalism brought into a series of bodies the societies on the rim of the world's largest ocean, but not the societies in the middle of that ocean or those Asian societies without a Pacific coastline. And with booming growth and year after year of peace and stability, commen-tators began to line up to proclaim the twenty-first century as the Asia Pacific's.

But history seems to enjoy embarrassing commentators. Even as the cry of the Asia Pacific century was taken up in elite talkfests and news magazines, the traffic was starting to decline on the trans-Pacific highway and to navigate anew along an old, long-forgotten, overgrown thoroughfare which traces its way along Asia's eastern and southern coastlines, from Japan in the north around to the Ara-bian Gulf in the west. Trade figures tell the story most starkly. In 1990, East Asia's trade with North America was just slightly less than its trade with the rest of Asia. As the prophets of the Asia Pacific century would have predicted, East Asia's trade with North America grew by three-and-a-quarter times between 1990 and 2007. The only problem was that East Asia's trade with the rest of Asia grew by six-and-a-quarter times over the same period. And the trends have been accelerating. Intra-Asian trade grew by 240 per cent during the 1990s, then by 280 per cent in the following decade. By the end of the first decade of the supposedly Asia Pacific century,

Asia's internal trade was more than two-and-a-quarter times the size of cross-Pacific trade. Investment trends are also likely to follow trade trends. As the developed world struggles with huge government debt, perceptions of sovereign risk and low interest rates in the years ahead, the emerging economies of Asia are likely to look to each other as the most rewarding investment destinations.

The new Indo-Pacific power highway is about more than just merchandise trade. Energy forms a large and growing proportion of the traffic. The Asian giants are responsible for over half of the growth in global energy demand since 1990. Between 1990 and 2007, China's oil consumption tripled, and India's increased by over two-and-a-quarter times. The International Energy Agency estimates that by 2030, China's demand for oil will have doubled again, and India's will have grown by almost two-and-a-half times. By 2030 India will be dependent on imports for over 80 per cent of its oil needs, and China will rely on imported oil for over 60 per cent of its. At the moment, the major Asian energy importers (add Japan and Korea to India and China) get over 80 per cent of their oil from the Gulf, while the Gulf provides over two-thirds of its natural gas to Asian markets. And because energy is so central to the ability of modern societies to function, governments and energy companies have been investing in their major suppliers and major markets. Japanese, Chinese and Indian financing has increased markedly in energy production in the Gulf, while the Gulf sheikhdoms have been eager to finance the growing network of giant oil refineries along Asia's southern and eastern coastlines.

Powerful countries have never been content just to let traders and financiers trace highways of mutual enrichment. Wherever money is being made, suspicions and rivalries flourish. And so it is with the Indo-Pacific. Trade in merchandise, energy and resources enrich the societies that take part, but the more a society is enriched by trade, the more vulnerable it becomes to its disruption. A country such as China, which needs energy to feed its booming economy, could be brought to its knees by a sudden cessation of energy deliveries. A supplier such as Saudi Arabia, which depends on oil revenues to underpin the fragile rule of its monarchy, could be thrown into chaos by a precipitous decline in the demand for its oil. And in a world where one country's vulnerability is another's opportunity, the flourishing of trade, energy, investment and resource flows will always attract military muscle.

The country that least trusts the United States Navy to maintain freedom of the seas is China. Unable and unwilling to challenge American naval power directly, Beijing has been developing port facilities along Asia's eastern and southern coastlines that could support a greater Chinese naval presence along the Indo-Pacific highway: on Hainan island, in the Paracel archipelago, at Kyauk Phyu in Myanmar, at Chittagong in Bangladesh, at Hambantota in Sri Lanka, and at Gwadar in Pakistan. Dubbed Beijing's 'string of pearls' strategy, these moves have worried India, and prompted vigorous discussions among its elites about how India might counter China's moves to strategically isolate it. Other countries that depend on Indo-Pacific trade flows, such as Japan, South Korea and Vietnam, have been gradually building their relationships with India, which is ideally positioned to dominate the Indian Ocean's seaways. All of these moves have so far been shadow boxing, because none of the Asian powers has the ability or will to displace the United States' overwhelming dominance of the Indo-Pacific sea lanes. But the giants' interest in the route has been registered. Since 2008, Chinese and Indian naval forces have been participating in a NATO-led task force protecting commercial shipping from Somali pirates in the Gulf of Aden.

The waning of the Asia Pacific era has also seen the fraying of the Asia Pacific's institutions. The original institutional expression of the trans-Pacific highway, APEC, has not had a clear vision – of purpose or of the future – for over a decade. The host of each annual leaders' meeting caucuses desperately in the lead-up months to find 'deliverables' – initiatives that sound grand enough to justify the region's leaders having spent a day in discussions yet uncontroversial enough to gain the unanimous consent required. Despite all this effort, APEC meetings become better known for subjecting world leaders to the humiliation of having to collectively disport themselves in front of photographers in a garish version of the national dress of the host country. The ASEAN Regional Forum, APEC's security counterpart, has sunk even deeper into obscurity. Far from serving as the arena for discussion of the Asia Pacific's security challenges, as its founders envisaged, it has become a formulaic exchange of national positions. The only sense in which it outdoes APEC is in the silliness of its tradition of requiring each national delegation to perform a karaoke-style cabaret act at the concluding dinner.

Yet as APEC and the ASEAN Regional Forum have slipped towards increasing irrelevance, a new regional institution has come into being. The East Asia Summit, founded in 2004, brings together the ten countries of South-East Asia – Vietnam, Laos, Cambodia, Burma, Thailand, Malaysia, Singapore, Indonesia, Brunei and the Philippines – with their four North-East Asian neighbours – China, South Korea, Japan and Russia – plus India, the United States, Australia and New Zealand. It is an organisation with no pretence to representing any trans-Pacific logic: the United States was not admitted until 2010 and there is no prospect of any other country in the Americas joining. But with the inclusion of India, the beginnings of an institutional recognition of an Indo-Pacific dynamic is clearly at play.

The Indo-Pacific power highway takes the pivot of world power away from the northern Pacific and northern Atlantic and shifts it to the southern and eastern coasts of the Asian landmass. It is here that the dynamism of the world economy will course, and where the rivalries and alignments that shape the way the world works will be played out. And one of the key arenas of the Indo-Pacific is South-East Asia. Any of the rising or established powers that can dominate South-East Asia will dominate the Indo-Pacific and beyond. In other words, the pivot of world affairs is moving inexorably closer to Australia's northern coastlines.

*

Most small countries that have survived and prospered know how to make hard-headed, unsentimental decisions about the waxing and waning of the power equations around them. The Thais, who survived relatively intact and uncolonised for hundreds of years in a pretty rough neighbourhood, describe the basic principles of their diplomacy as 'waving grass': being flexible enough to bend according to the prevailing currents of power. Australia has been just as unsentimental as the tides of power turned. When it became obvious that Britain had neither the ability nor the inclination to protect Australia in the midst of World War II, Canberra didn't hesitate to ally closely with Britain's great strategic competitor in the region, the United States. After the war, London's protests at being left out of alliance negotiations between Australia, the United States and New Zealand caused Australian leaders not a moment's pause or regret as they signed the ANZUS Treaty.

To this way of thinking, a shifting power equation should be met with the same pragmatism that small countries have fallen back upon for most of history. The currents and highways of power should be assessed with a dispassionate gaze, and loyalties and commitments realigned to the country's interest without any hint of sentimentality or hesitation. But the problem is that world affairs is no longer like a horse race, with a clear ordering of power and precedence. This is a messy, uncertain, heteropolar world, of variable geometries of power that interact, amplify and retard each other in different ways. It is also evolving quickly. The task of understanding what all this means for a country like Australia is made doubly hard by the fact that for the past sixty years, the power ordering of the world has been incredibly simple, clear and mostly uncontroversial – perhaps more so than at any other period in the existence of a global system of international affairs. To be catapulted suddenly into the opposite – a complex, evolving, ambiguous dynamic – is deeply challenging for this country, as it is for others like it. And all this at a time when power's highways have moved much closer to our shores.

The psychology
of power

4

The formal coronation of the Mughal Emperor Aurangzeb took place in the shimmering heat of mid-June at Delhi's Red Fort in 1659. The new emperor took the title 'Alamgir' – 'conqueror of the world' – and proclaimed himself as brilliant as the sun. The centrepiece of the ceremony was the incredible Peacock Throne, encrusted with 108 rubies, 116 emeralds, hundreds of pearls, and the largest known diamond in the world, the Koh-i-Noor. The ceremony lasted all day, and involved Aurangzeb giving elaborate gifts

of money, weapons, gems and animals to the princes and princesses of the empire. The gifts he received from the assembled embassies included a huge diamond, two rubies, nine emeralds, ten Arabian pearls, one sapphire, five elephants and five horses saddled in gold and silver. The coronation was followed by two and a half months of festivities, featuring nightly fireworks 'more brilliant than the stars' and boats decorated with flowers and torches floating along the Jamuna River.

The man who ascended the Peacock Throne was the third son of Emperor Shah Jahan, who commissioned the Taj Mahal. Aurangzeb had spent much of his childhood as a hostage of his grandfather, the Emperor Jahangir, after Shah Jahan had tried to depose him. Tutored by a noted Islamic scholar, he spent part of his teens as an ascetic Muslim monk. Much of his spare time he spent hand-copying the Koran and decorating devotional Muslim skull-caps. Aurangzeb had a difficult relationship with his father, who favoured his oldest son, despite Aurangzeb's successes commanding Shah Jahan's armies. When Shah Jahan fell ill, Aurangzeb fought his father and brothers for the throne. His victory left three of his brothers dead and his father under house arrest, where he remained until his death.

Aurangzeb ruled for fifty years and extended the Mughal Empire further than any other emperor, from the mountains of Afghanistan to the plains of southern India. But the empire he built was a brittle edifice. Unlike the great Mughal emperors before him, who had adapted Islam to accommodate India's religious diversity, Aurangzeb was a doctrinaire Sunni Muslim. On gaining power he banned music and gambling, banished prostitutes from court and re-imposed the 'jizyah', or Muslim tax on unbelievers. His reign was marked by the destruction of Hindu temples, the enslavement of Christian communities, and brutal attempts to eradicate the Sikh religion. His expansion of the Mughal Empire came at tragic cost. Aurangzeb built an enormous army, but his religious intolerance sparked rebellions among the non-Muslim troops he relied on so heavily. His constant campaigns cost his army over 100 000 lives. His mobile campaign headquarters alone consisted of 500 000 staff and followers, 50 000 camels and 30 000 elephants. The imperial coffers were soon empty, and India was stripped of its surplus food and wealth. Aurangzeb's legacy was a huge empire beset inside and out by implacable enemies, a royal family riven by murderous intrigue, a society destabilised by bitter sectarianism, and an impoverished country vulnerable to European encroachment. Less than a hundred years after Aurangzeb's death, the boundaries of the Mughal Empire could be reached in less than a day's walk from the Red Fort. The shattering of his empire allowed the entry of the British, and within two hundred years of his elaborate coronation the Koh-i-Noor became just one of Britain's Crown Jewels.

For most of human history, few matters have been more important than the character of kings. Their predilections and decisions have built or destroyed empires, and yet rarely have they been chosen according to their abilities. For that very reason, royal families have long tried to leaven the lottery of birth with elaborate programs of grooming and preparation for likely monarchs. The very best scholars are hired to tutor princes and princesses, the best warriors to hone prowess and judgement, great artists to refine taste, theologians and philosophers to burnish morals. And more often than not, prospective monarchs are given command – of a department or a campaign – to familiarise them with the pressures of responsibility. But the best grooming in the world won't make the difference between a good and a bad king. Frederick II of Prussia was one of the leading authors and composers of his day, but a strategic blunderer who would have lost his kingdom but for the sudden death of the Russian Empress. The founder of China's brilliant Ming Dynasty began life as a orphaned peasant reliant on the charity of a monastery.

The reason is that power has unpredictable effects on people. No one is fully prepared for the sudden reality of command and responsibility. Ultimately what determines how a prince or princess reacts to the throne is character – an inner appreciation of what is important, how relationships work, and what can be ventured for what stakes. The biographies of the powerful suggest that one potent shaper of the character of leaders is their own experience of power. Have they been on the rough end of power, used capriciously or arrogantly? Have they admired or been repulsed by the corruptive warp of power? Have they seen the wise use of power to bring about positive change? Aurangzeb's childhood and adolescence, shaped as they were by the twin dynamics of the capricious power of monarchs and the consoling power of Islam, shaped how he as emperor would use his enormous power once on the Peacock Throne.

If it's hard to predict the effects of power on individuals, it's twice as hard to predict how countries will respond to rapid enrichment and influence – or sudden disempowerment. Who would have predicted that a society founded on liberty and the rejection of diplomatic intrigue would ultimately become a superpower deeply involved in the geopolitics of all regions of the earth? Or that a country known for its musical, philosophical and theological brilliance would almost self-immolate in an orgy of racial genocide? Or that an empire founded on deep paranoia about internal and external threats would simply relinquish long-held confrontations and dominions, leaving the trigger to the world's largest nuclear arsenal untouched? As with kings, the best guide for how countries will respond to power lies in examining their own past experience of power.

Status shock

Each one of Aurangzeb's subjects was born into a precise position in a strict social hierarchy, and died in the same role. His Hindu subjects were all bound by the ancient caste system, which permitted contact with some people and not others, determined professions and privileges, and placed each soul in a particular space in the moral universe. Aurangzeb's Muslim subjects, despite their religion's strongly egalitarian injunctions, were no less bound by hierarchy. The Mughals were conquerors, and therefore very conscious of the ruling position in society; most of the other Muslims were Hindu converts, unable to fully escape their caste backgrounds, and were treated accordingly by others. Hindu conceptions of caste hierarchy spread beyond the subcontinent, animating the great Majapahit Empire based in eastern Java and extending across the Malay Peninsula, Borneo, Sumatra, and to Bali. Majapahit was to decline and be replaced by Muslim kingdoms, but the hierarchical cosmology of the Hindus, especially the relationship between the ruler's asceticism and spiritual prowess to terrestrial power, remained a powerful influence on Malay society. Sanskritic culture, art and philosophies also heavily influenced the earliest kingdoms of mainland South-East Asia, with enduring effects on their societies.

Aurangzeb's contemporary in China was the Emperor Kangxi, who consolidated and extended the Qing Dynasty over the course of a remarkable 61-year reign. His subjects were as closely bound in a hierarchical order as Aurangzeb's. Although they were Manchurian, the Qing adopted and enforced the Confucian philosophy of society, which premised the order and stability of the vast Chinese Empire on each member behaving according to the precise ranking and role they had been born into. Confucius had specified the key principles of behaviour of all in society as well as how they should relate to each other: superiors to inferiors with forbearance; inferiors to superiors with deference. The Confucian concept of a detailed and fixed social hierarchy stretched into Korea, where the Joseon Dynasty ruled, and into northern Vietnam, then under the rule of the Trinh Dynasty. Seventeenth-century Japan was ruled by the powerful Tokugawa shoguns who instituted a clear hierarchy that placed samurai warriors above other professions. Even within the samurai there were hundreds of distinctions and rankings, the prerogatives of each determined by a brutal code of honour.

Whatever their philosophical or cultural roots, whatever the borrowings and adaptations, whatever systems of justification and enforcement they relied upon, there are remarkable similarities between the hierarchical social systems of India, China, Korea, Japan and much of South-East Asia. In all, infinite gradations of inequality pervaded society, through complex systems of birth, rank and occupation, in the highly detailed language of honorifics and titles, in the ritualised and exacting social practice and etiquette, and through religious cosmology, literature, art, architecture and education. Hierarchical systems had no universal rules or absolutes of good and evil; all behaviour was to be judged relative to the status of the people involved and the situation at hand. Those with higher status had greater latitude of action than the lower orders.

The people who occupied the serried ranks in Asian societies paid close attention to the maintenance of the dignity, esteem and prerogatives of their status, and all were aware of the terrible consequences that faced those who stepped outside of their social bounds. Enforcement was top-down, with those of higher rank determined to maintain their separation from and superiority over those below. In each society, the elite developed highly ritualised forms of etiquette, dress, behaviour, learning and religious observance, which both distinguished them from lower classes and served as a constant justification of their higher rank. Their manners, cultivation and fastidiousness were what separated them from the coarse and boorish lower orders, and over the course of centuries the civilisation of each society's elites came to be seen by that community as the pinnacle of human achievement. Civilisation was viewed as society's progress away from humanity's base animality, and became as hierarchical and relative among societies as within them. The civilisational glories embodied in culture, manners and empire became the core expression of the self-assurance of societies, and myths of civilisational superiority were carefully tended and embedded in official scholarship over centuries. The Emperor of China insisted on ritual demonstrations of his superiority to the rulers of surrounding societies because it was essential to his supremacy within China – and to the whole intricate hierarchy he sat atop. Aurangzeb's self-title 'Alamgir', conqueror of the world, was intended for domestic, not foreign consumption.

It was the Chinese and Indian civilisations that were most convinced of their superiority. Both were huge in population and landmass, with great wealth and dynamism, and continuous literate cultures stretching back to antiquity. The Chinese could further boast centuries of unified rule over the vast and populous Han civilisation and beyond, and a vibrant history of technological innovation. Both Chinese and Indian civilisations derived great self-regard from their cultural influences beyond their territorial boundaries: in writing and literature, cosmology and philosophy, epicure, art and knowledge. Their cultural influence was consensual, not forced, being carried beyond China and India by scholars, traders and monks. It found fertile soil in societies that were equally hierarchically minded – such as Hindu conceptions of untouchable professions that were carried to Japan by Buddhist monks and even now condemn communities of ethnic Japanese to live as 'burakumin', unclean outcasts. The response of smaller societies was to absorb and indigenise Sinic and Indic influences, and their hierarchic mindsets led them to insist that what they had interpreted and adapted

98

was ultimately superior to what they had absorbed. The Japanese, for instance, believed in the unique perfection of their own culture and an almost mystic conception of social unity based in the divine origin of the ancient, unbroken line of emperors. The implacable self-esteem that imbued Asian societies was not an affectation or arrogance, but a collective psychology and cosmology fundamental to social order and stability.

Medieval European Christendom's social order was no less intricately hierarchical than those of the societies of Asia. The great German historian von Gierke described medieval Europeans' vision of the unity of humanity under the Catholic Church and Holy Roman Empire as:

> a vaulted dome of an organically articulated structure of
> human society. In Church and Empire the Total Body is
> a manifold and graduated system of partial bodies, each
> of which, though itself a Whole, necessarily demands a
> connection with the larger Whole.

But the European explorers' discovery of other ancient civilisations that were culturally and religiously self-contained had shattered Christendom's belief in a single human story that unfolded seamlessly according to a divine plan. European societies' march towards a post-hierarchical social order began with the Protestant challenge to the authority of the Catholic Church, the spread of humanist ideals, and the gradual advance of printing and literacy. The crumbling of the authority of the Catholic Church and the Holy Roman Empire ushered in a system in which sovereigns and republics jostled against each other as equals, each living on its prowess or luck and never expecting or giving any more deference than they received. As historian Michael Howard puts it, Europe shifted away from:

> Dantesque gradations in which secular, ecclesiastical and
> divine hierarchies paralleled and reflected one another [to] a
> new Newtonian concept ... in which order was preserved by
> the relationships between the states themselves, as the order
> of the universe was preserved by the relationships between
> the planets.

Europeans' rapid empowerment by the industrial revolution and the great divergence between their numbers and their contribution to world economic output occurred at a time when socially they were leaving behind rigid systems of status and rank, of feudal privilege and obligation, of divine sanction, and of beliefs that social roles determined human destiny.

Asia's empires had initially dealt with European explorers, traders and missionaries with a mixture of condescension, curiosity and contempt. They were granted small privileges which could be capriciously removed. They were never left in any doubt that they were dealing with superior civilisations, which had no need of what Europe could offer, but were prepared to allow Europe access to their own cultural bounties. But as Europe's courting became more insistent, it began to disturb the self-confidence of Asia's societies. They started to draw inwards to try to maintain their own social integrity and harmony. Contact with foreigners was drastically quarantined, often to islands or districts close to peripheral trading ports. But this was never going to satisfy European societies, growing ever more confident in their coercive abilities, ever more convinced of their cultural and racial superiority, and ever more voracious in their search for markets, raw materials and luxury commodities.

Never has history's course been so profoundly redirected so casually and so inadvertently. Britain's slow assertion of control over India came at the cost of just a handful of British lives, at least until the Sepoy uprising of 1857, which has been estimated to have

resulted in 2000 British military and civilian casualties. The Opium
Wars and relief of Beijing came at the cost of 3000 dead and wounded
British and imperial troops. Admiral Perry's demarche in Tokyo Bay
cost not a single American life. The French gained control of Indo-
china at an estimated cost of 2100 killed and wounded. Dutch control of Indonesia has been calculated to have cost 8000 Dutch lives.
Most of these conquests began as no more than demands for greater
access for traders and missionaries, but soon developed into confrontations over the status and privileges of Europeans in Asia. For
the Europeans it was about little more than enrichment and strategic
rivalries between themselves. For the Asians it meant no less than a
brutal and enduring rending of the myths and beliefs that had sustained their sense of social and cosmological order for millennia.

The Europeans and Americans, who were progressively leaving
behind their own sensibilities of rank and social ritual, seemed only
dimly aware of the impact of their actions. The off-handed arrogance
and disdainful lack of courtesy of the Europeans and Americans was
profoundly disturbing to Asian elites accustomed to elaborately ritualised interactions. The immunities that the foreigners demanded,
and the impunity with which they acted, placed them above the
highest ranks in Asian societies. What was most astounding to
Asians was that these large, dirty, boorish foreigners were so much
more technologically and materially advanced than their own civilisations, in which they had invested so much pride. The profound
self-assurance of Asia's great civilisations in their superiority in technology and science, theology and philosophy, scholarship and literature, wealth and potency, was casually punctured by the sudden
evidence of European dominance. The Mughals' scientific and technological backwardness was rudely demonstrated on the battlefield.
China's great material gifts to humanity – tea, silk, gunpowder –
were soon being manufactured to greater quality, quantity and prof-
itability by the European empires. Hindus' beliefs in their superior

spirituality were challenged by missionaries' condemnation of their idolatry and social practices. The empires of the Orient that had long dazzled visitors with their opulence and wealth gradually fell into deep, enduring poverty.

The psychic shock from the Europeans' sudden and effortless ascendancy was so deep and enduring not because Asian societies were egalitarian, but because they were fundamentally hierarchical. There were pre-existing prejudices in Asian societies that seemed to confirm the supremacy of Europeans and Americans. Asian cosmologies had a cyclic view of history, of the rise of civilisations and the decline of others, with their respective fortunes reflecting not only divine preferences but also genetic, social and cultural strengths and weaknesses. The sudden dominance of Europeans and Americans set off self-perceptions of decadence and decline, triggering rolling social and political revolutions that brought an end to Asia's imperial societies. Elitist conceptions of the superiority of lighter to darker skin were well established in India, China, Japan and Korea long before white foreigners appeared in force. Existing prejudices and the initial deference of the natives probably had a major influence in reinforcing the growing belief in Europe and its settler colonies of a hierarchy of human races, with white people at the apex. But in Asian societies, hierarchical sensibilities chafed at the swagger and condescension of white people. The inhuman brutality of both colonised and colonisers during Asia's many imperial rebellions came from deep forces of cultural and racial resentment and revenge.

The ultimate trauma came from the realisation that in order to match and throw off the invaders' superior material power, to take back control of their own destinies, Asian societies would have to borrow heavily from Western civilisation, where before they had been so self-sufficient and comfortable in their own cultural systems. A deep self-loathing replaced cultural self-confidence: ancient traditions were no longer what distinguished the Asian empires, but what retarded them. For the Japanese, national redemption meant not only learning quickly and well from Europe and America, but rejecting and destroying the Chinese world order. Japan's wars against China, Korea and ultimately all of South-East Asia were as much motivated by a rejection of the world in which it had existed for centuries as it was by material gains. The savagery of the fighting during Japan's wars in Asia can not be explained by military logic alone: deep civilisational imperatives were at work. The shock to China of defeat and invasion at the hands of what it had regarded as an inferior, derivative society was far greater than its humiliation by Westerners. Mortification at being compared to other colonised or humiliated Asian societies long predated any feelings of Asian solidarity against imperialism.

But for all who wanted to reject ancient traditions and learn quickly from the West, there were those in every Asian society who argued that redemption lay in rejecting foreign influences and cleaving ever more closely to the pure ideals of their own society. Paradoxically, while the colonisers treated natives on a day-to-day basis with contempt, condescension and evangelism, Western scholars began to discover the ancient glories of Asia's civilisations. Here was evidence of Asia's greatness rather than received wisdom and myth. At a slightly later date came a great admiration for the 'superiorities' of Asian cultures: the aesthetics and design, the rationality of the Japanese, the great foresight and planning of the Chinese. The result was an enduring schizophrenia in Asian societies between tradition and modernity, authenticity and adaptation.

Strange new world

In the scale of Asia's long history, the colonisers came and went in the blink of an eye. The most tenacious were the Spanish, the Portuguese and the Dutch, whose rule lasted centuries. The British,

French, Americans and Japanese lasted just decades. But despite their brevity compared to other invasions, the European, American and Japanese colonisers couldn't be as easily absorbed culturally or digested psychologically by Asia's civilisations. Even after their sudden departure from most of Asia in the decade between 1947 and 1957, their legacy remained – within Asian societies, and outside in the international order in which they had to make their way.

In particular the Europeans left behind the casing into which every society had to fit itself – the state. With its absolute borders, its national flags, anthems and currency, this was very much a European invention, and for all of their sophistication and antiquity, most Asian societies had to contort themselves to fit. Most pressingly, the leaders of Asia's new states had to craft meaning from circumstance. The uncomfortable truth for many was that the countries they led were in outline, administrative structure, and composition merely the continuations of former colonies. What became India in 1947 had never existed as a single entity prior to the completion of the raj across the sub-continent in the late nineteenth century. Indonesia made even less sense without admitting that its borders were those that the Dutch had drawn around their Malay empire. Arbitrary borders often meant the additional challenge of forging unity from diversity. The new countries were mosaics of different ethnicities and religions, while the new borders also separated previous social and cultural groupings. What became Laos was the result of French imperial administrative convenience, and in the end many more ethnic Lao became citizens of Thailand than of Laos. The people of northern Sumatra were divided by an Anglo-Dutch compact from their ethnic, religious and linguistic kin across the Malacca Straits: the former were united as Indonesians with the very different Ambonese, while the latter became Malaysians. Then the independence generation had to find initiative amidst inertia. During the colonial period, history was something that was done to Asian societies, not something they made. New, viable nations faced the therapeutic challenge of restoring initiative and dignity to peoples who had faced the condescension and arbitrary rule of Europeans and Americans.

Ultimately the leaders of Asia's new countries reached back into history to justify and give a sense of permanence and inevitability to the states they were building. Gandhi and Nehru fabricated the idea of an Indian civilisation and spirituality that transcended and embraced the sub-continent's vast linguistic, religious and ethnic diversity. In deposing the emperor in 1911, Republican China had to fall back on civilisational conceptions of unity and continuity with the past. These were intensified by the Nationalists' and Communists' struggle for ascendancy and authenticity; Chiang Kai-shek's determination to take as many as possible of China's imperial art treasures with him as he fled to Taiwan was motivated by authenticity rather than aesthetics. The Indonesian nationalists also had to borrow liberally from across the cultural history of the archipelago, to first construct a people for whose freedom they were fighting, then to urge them to fight for independence, and then to fight internally against those who challenged Indonesia's unity. Wars for reunification in Korea and Vietnam burnished distinctive, historically rooted national ideologies. The constant invocation of the glories of the pre-colonial past grafted a particularly prickly form of nationalist pride on to underlying hierarchical mindsets.

The era of decolonisation seemed to sweep away many of the most obvious sources of humiliation. Biological conceptions of racial supremacy were in headlong retreat before the West's revulsion at the genocide of World War II. Also in lockstep retreat was the condescending 'standard of civilisation' in international law, the level of sophistication which non-Western societies had to reach before they could qualify for full statehood and membership of international society. Suddenly the onus of justification was on white countries that still controlled non-white societies, and nationalist leaders were meeting their former colonisers on equal terms. The new states were quickly admitted to the United Nations and other global agencies with the status, privileges and immunities equivalent to European and American countries.

But as they grew used to their formal equalities, the informal and structural biases in how the world worked became more obvious and galling. All of Asia's new states were only too aware of their own poverty and fragility, in stark contrast to the strength and wealth of their former colonisers. A developmental hierarchy replaced the racial hierarchy. Asian states were more fragile and poor because they were less developed – but if they followed Western or Soviet trajectories and advice, they would inevitably reach similarly advanced levels. Asians might have assumed full control over national treasuries and currencies, but it was hard to believe they were fully in control of their economic destinies as they were blown and buffeted by the currents of the global economy centred in the Atlantic. Their superior numbers and equal voting rights were unable to change any of this through global institutions. An Asian became secretary-general of the United Nations in 1961 (as part of a rotating arrangement among the world's regions), but the Europeans and Americans kept the top job in the global institutions with the money – the International Monetary Fund and the World Bank – firmly to themselves.

The rules, languages and meeting-places of world affairs had all been designed and agreed before the Asians arrived. A great edifice of international law had been constructed at a time when most of humanity was living in colonies, and there was no legislative process through which to change international law now that the peoples of Asia were in control of their own states. Europeans and Americans needed little preparation to work internationally, but Asians needed to master foreign languages, rules, etiquette, precedents and procedures. As the People's Republic of China found out, these could be easily manipulated by those in the know to exclude countries they opposed or disdained. Europeans and Americans, despite their historical propensity to fight each other, were much more willing to trust each other than Asians. Their intelligence-sharing arrangements and detailed, binding alliance agreements were confined to fellow Western societies only. Where Asians were involved, confidences were rare and alliances were vague, unequal and inconsequential. The great gulfs in strength, wealth and confidence couldn't help but colour the relationships between the Atlantic powers and their Asian allies.

Roles and reconciliations

The inequalities and indignities that Asian countries faced internationally sat uncomfortably with the pride in their civilisational history they were fostering internally. Their response was a judgemental cast of mind and a predisposition to interpret the way the world worked as immoral. The anthropologist Partha Chatterjee observes that even under colonial rule, Asian societies preserved their inner sense of cultural and spiritual distinctiveness and superiority, even while they conceded the technological, military and economic dominance of Europeans and Americans. Their sense of moral purpose was burnished during struggles for independence, and further honed as they experienced the gap between their formal sovereign equalities and the realities of where the power and wealth were concentrated in the world.

The sense of principled objection to the world was strongest among the largest. Despite the shock of colonial subjugation, China, India and eventually Indonesia were still aware that each of them accounted for a substantial fraction of humanity and human disadvantage, as well sizeable proportions of the earth's surface. Neither China nor India had relinquished their pride in their technological, cultural and spiritual contributions to humanity. Both had a strong belief that the wealth of their societies had been plundered by the colonialists, and that they had been left poor and backward while Europe and America had grown wealthy and powerful. Their Confucian and Brahmin elites had bitterly resented the racism and condescension of the colonisers. An inner sense of exceptionalism led India's Congress Party and China's Communist Party to see their own struggles against colonialist invaders as at the vanguard of a world-wide struggle of oppressed peoples. India's first prime minister, Jawaharlal Nehru, drew a direct line from India's spiritualist essence through the Congress movement's non-violent resistance to British rule to a catalytic role for India in leading the movement to establish a moral and just world order. For the independence leaders – Nehru, Zhou, Sukarno, Ho – the principles of struggling for a more just world became extensions of their own personalities, imbued with their own substantial charisma.

The major element in the international attitudes of these very different countries and leaders was complete opposition to a world controlled by a handful of countries that had become wealthy by colonising others. They soon found common cause in their refusal to compromise their hard-won independence by becoming satellites of either of the superpowers. Indonesia organised a conference of 29 Asian and African countries in April 1955 which called for a reduction in mounting Cold War tensions and denounced colonialism in all of its manifestations. This was to develop into a caucus group of poor former colonies that used the United Nations as a forum to campaign for an end to white rule in southern Africa and the Israeli occupation of Palestinian territories, and for the equalisation of wealth between rich and poor countries. By the 1970s the United Nations had become an arena of bitter confrontation between the United States and its allies and a Third World bloc increasingly militant in its demands for greater justice. But while the non-aligned countries' huge voting majorities controlled the General Assembly agenda and passed more and more uncompromising resolutions, the world's inequities remained and gradually widened. The United States and some of its allies became gradually estranged from the United Nations and its subsidiary bodies, walking out of UNESCO, the International Labour Organisation and negotiations on the Law of the Sea. A growing frustration at the apparent impotence of their demands, despite numerical majorities, led to a steady increase in the stridency of the rhetoric of the developing world and a deepening sense amongst them that the global order was deeply unjust.

But for all of their principled opposition to power politics, Asia's new states were remarkably ready to resort to armed force. Despite Nehru's rhetoric of morality, justice and non-violence, India launched attacks on Pakistan in 1947, 1965 and 1971, and invaded the Portuguese enclave of Goa in 1961. In 1954, China and India agreed on Five Principles of Peaceful Coexistence (mutual respect for territorial integrity and sovereignty; mutual non-aggression; mutual non-interference; equality and mutual benefit; and peaceful coexistence) which remain the central doctrine of Chinese foreign policy. Yet by 1962 they were at war, and have been strategic rivals ever since. In addition to India, China fought against South Korea (1950–1953), the Soviet Union (1969) and Vietnam (1979). During the 1960s, Beijing became a major sponsor of Communist insurgencies in a range of countries in South-East and South Asia. China detonated its first atomic device in 1964; India followed in 1974. Indonesia resorted to force in its confrontation with Singapore and Malaysia, and during its invasion of East Timor in 1975. Nor did their determination to remain at arms-length from the superpowers last long. China revealed its Treaty of Friendship, Alliance and Mutual Assistance with the Soviet Union in February 1950, while India's anxiety at American and Chinese support for Pakistan led to an increasingly close relationship with Moscow. By the end of the 1970s, the independent Asian dream of bringing about a more just world through principled action and diplomacy was further away than ever. The wealth gap between the West and Asia's new states was as great as it had been at the end of the 1940s, the rules and institutions of world affairs were useless for bringing about real change, and Asia's champions of moral change were more isolated than they had ever been.

The sudden collapse of the Soviet Union in the late 1980s seemed to only emphasise the ascendancy of the West and the marginalisation of Asia. Japan, the world's second-largest economy, had bowed to American brow-beating and accepted a devaluation of the dollar against the yen, and was soon to be roundly criticised by Washington for staying within the bounds of its American-imposed peace constitution and failing to send forces to help eject Iraq from Kuwait. Despite the dramatic puncturing of Japan's economic growth rates, Tokyo still agreed to underwrite a good deal of the first Gulf War. China's massacre of students in Tiananmen Square in June 1989 had returned it to its 1960s pariah status. The authoritarianism of its government was made even more obvious by sudden transitions from dictatorship to democracy in the Philippines, Taiwan, South Korea and Thailand – not to mention the former Soviet Union and Eastern Europe. Rising agitation against Indonesia's rule in East Timor, and Jakarta's invariably heavy-handed responses, deepened its international isolation. When India detonated nuclear weapons in 1998 – quickly followed by Pakistan – it faced a wave of condemnation and sanctions. A financial crisis swept across eastern Asia in 1997, turning back decades of economic progress and giving great schadenfreude to all those who had criticised and felt threatened by the state-directed capitalism of the Asian tigers. And all the while the West got stronger, wealthier, more convinced in the superiority of its political and economic philosophies, and increasingly willing to reorder the world according to its tastes.

Power and prejudice

Cancun lies at the end of the Yucatan Peninsula, at the point where Mexico stretches deepest into the Caribbean. Graced on one side by the glistening waters of the Caribbean and on the other by the Nichupté Lagoon, this ancient town has come to be known as the 'Mayan Riviera'. Honeymooners and holidaymakers crowd its beaches and streets throughout the year, drawn by its exotic mix of history, outdoor sports, wildlife and reputation for extravagant luxury. It was to Cancun in September 2003 that Mexican President Vicente Fox invited the trade ministers of the 147 members of the World Trade Organization for a new round of talks aimed at promoting global free trade.

As they flew into Cancun, few delegates from wealthy countries had many doubts that these talks would unfold according to a well-rehearsed pattern. The United States and the European Union had decided on an agenda for discussions in Geneva the previous week and circulated it to all participants. The lack of consultation or time for other countries to respond or prepare didn't surprise anyone. Ever since global trade talks began in 1947, it had been the United States, eventually joined by Europe and Japan, that determined the nature of each round of free trade measures. These two countries plus one region accounted for such a great proportion of all global economic activity that every other country had little choice but to accede to what they eventually decided. Smaller economies might win marginal changes or even exemptions, but none had seriously tried to shape the agenda. The efforts of Australia and other agricultural exporters to get the Japanese to drop their agriculture tariffs and the Americans and Europeans to stop subsidising their farmers had been particularly unsuccessful.

The Cancun meeting started as expected. The first three days saw facilitators appointed to shepherd key issues through the

111

negotiations, Cambodia and Nepal admitted as WTO members, and African countries unsuccessfully try to place distorted global cotton markets onto the agenda. But by day four, when the facilitators began to float the text of a possible 'Cancun Declaration', conference chairman Luis Ernesto Derbez and WTO Director-General Supachai Panitchpakdi began to sense that there was something seriously wrong.

A group of developing countries had been saying for some time that they would abandon the talks if agricultural trade liberalisation and other issues of great interest to them were not up for serious negotiation, but no one had taken them seriously. Such countries had been complaining about the Euro-American-Japanese shut-out of agricultural trade reform for decades, but they always seemed to meekly play along in the end. The countries at the head of this push included Brazil, China, India, South Africa, Mexico and Thailand. They were particularly annoyed that the European-American agenda had given special prominence to freeing up investment rules – a measure set to favour the big European, American and Japanese multinationals – while paying lip service to talks on agriculture and the trade in clothing and fabric.

By the time the bargaining stalled on day five, the significance of what had happened began to sink in. The developing countries had made good on their threat to bring talks to a halt if their concerns were not met. American and European threats and bribes had not been able to break the unity of the opposition. Whereas in the past developing countries had caved because they wanted to avoid being seen as the wreckers of global trade talks, this time it was the Americans and Europeans who were more worried about the talks failing. For the first time in over half a century, the Americans, Europeans and Japanese had not been able to hammer out an agreement among themselves that would automatically become the global trade norm. This time, at 4 o'clock on the morning of 15 September 2003, they knew that they no longer accounted for a large enough slice of the global economy for the old logic to apply.

For all their moral certainty and reforming passion, the countries of the Third World had little effect on reshaping the global economy when they had tried previously, through establishing the United Nations Conference on Trade and Development in the 1960s or through fighting for a New International Economic Order in the 1970s. But at Cancun, moral certainty and reforming passion had given way to self-assurance, clear self-interest, and comfort with the dark arts of multilateral bargaining. By 2003 China, Brazil, India and Indonesia were no longer demandeurs; they were the growth dynamos of the world economy, and along with Russia they would soon be given their own collective acronym – BRIC – by Goldman Sachs. Many of Asia's rapidly developing countries no longer had any illusions that the world's wealthy countries would ever voluntarily match their concerned rhetoric about the problems of the Third World with meaningful action. The response of the United States and the International Monetary Fund to the Asian financial crisis was a psychological watershed. Instead of concern and real support for the crisis-hit Asian tigers, America and the IMF adopted the attitude of Victorian-era parents: judgemental, patronising tough love. The answer for Asia's countries was to opt for much greater self-reliance: piling up huge reserves of US dollars, building regional stabilisation arrangements, and taking a much closer interest in how negotiations on the international economy would affect their own prosperity.

The 1990s also saw China, India, and other large developing countries evolve from being defensive, moralising and ineffective in international agencies to a much greater level of engagement, pragmatism and effectiveness. China's progress from pariah status to international deal-maker in the twenty years after Tiananmen Square has been nothing short of remarkable. Despite its permanent seat on the UN Security Council and major roles in the World Bank, Asian Development Bank and IMF, China had traditionally been suspicious of international agencies – and justifiably so. It was organisations such as the UN that had denied China admission until 1971, and had been key mechanisms for its marginalisation in the world. Even after China took up its seat at the UN, it faced a steady barrage of criticisms from UN agencies over its human rights practices. The UN experience was revisited in the 1990s when the United States and Europe used China's bid to join the WTO as a lever to extract a range of trade concessions from Beijing. China regarded multilateral settings as places where its critics could gang up and force it to do things it opposed, and so it much preferred dealing individually with other countries. It had additional reasons to be wary during the 1990s, as the United States and a range of other countries began calling for the use of international agencies as a way to 'socialise' China into the rules of the system.

The key mechanisms for China's intended socialisation were a range of regional bodies: APEC, the ASEAN Regional Forum and later leaders-level meetings within ASEAN. Initially Beijing had to be shoehorned into APEC and the ASEAN Regional Forum, and spent the initial years in these bodies silent and suspicious. But gradually its diplomats awoke to just how comfortable these meetings were. Based firmly on the ASEAN operating principles of consensus, avoidance of controversy, and opposition to criticising or interfering in each other's internal affairs, these regional agencies offered China a range of advantages with no risks. By the turn of the century, Beijing had used ASEAN, APEC and the ASEAN Regional Forum to reassure its Asian neighbours, soften its image, and build trade and investment linkages into the region. Suddenly China was receiving accolades that were out of all proportion to the costs it incurred: not devaluing its currency during the Asian financial crisis; softening its stance on its territorial claims in the South

China Sea; negotiating security and free trade agreements with all of South-East Asia's countries. The uncomfortable truth was that China had instead used international agencies to socialise the world to its rise at least as effectively as the world had used international agencies to socialise China.

India's campaign to end its isolation after the 1998 nuclear tests has been no less remarkable. Its diplomats were effective and uncompromising in using the double standards of the Nuclear Non-Proliferation Treaty to argue that the West was employing 'nuclear apartheid' against New Delhi. No chance was missed to point out India's superior non-proliferation record to those of China, Russia and France – all accepted as nuclear weapons states by the treaty. And after the September 11 terrorist attacks, India was highly effective at drawing parallels between the jihadist terrorism that threatened America and Europe and its own long-running battle against extremists based in Kashmir and Pakistan. Within a decade, the United States had signed a civil nuclear co-operation agreement with India, in effect accepting it as a de facto nuclear weapons state. The Nuclear Suppliers Group, which had previously denied uranium sales to any country outside of the treaty rules, voted to exempt India from those rules. No longer is India habitually hyphenated with Pakistan. Indonesia too has quietly worked to rehabilitate its image after the 1999 East Timor crisis and the terrorist attacks between 2002 and 2007. Its growing economic and security linkages with other countries of Asia and the Pacific show how effective it has been. Now Indonesia is a key player in the G20 and a standard-bearer for democracy and counter-terrorism.

These experiences changed countries that were once marginal and hectoring voices in international negotiations into hard-headed and resourceful multilateral operators, willing to take hard decisions, able to caucus among themselves, and increasingly aware of their ability to block initiatives they disagree with.

The honour of a nation

But for all of their growing prominence and clout, there is still a great deal that concerns Asia's giants about the world. China and India each account for close to one-fifth of the world's population, and neither believes it has a voice on global issues even closely commensurate with its demographic size. As they daily become more dependent on energy and resources shipped from the rest of the world, they become increasingly aware that all of the prime energy and resources real estate – 'tier one assets' in resource sector jargon – was snapped up long ago either by huge multinational mining companies or by equally big state-sector resource and energy agencies. China in particular is nervous that the country that patrols the oceans through which its trade and energy sails is also the country most worried about its rising strategic challenge.

Furthermore, despite all of their dynamism and growth, the world keeps telling China and India that they are not yet adequate. The United States and its allies repeatedly proclaim that China needs to become a 'responsible stakeholder' as it assumes a position of power and authority in the world. The phrase may make for slick diplomacy, but for Beijing it carries implicit warnings not to tamper with existing rules, as well as an explicit claim that China is not and has not been acting responsibly. India faces more infrequent judgements – such as when US President Barak Obama admonished it for not taking a harder line on human rights failings of other countries in a speech to the Lok Sabha in November 2010 – but when they are made, they rankle.

Despite their growing power, Asia's giants are still 'developing' countries. India is home to one-third of the world's poor. Tens of millions of Chinese live in abject poverty. Despite being the world's second largest economy, the average wealth level of people in China is around that of the average Angolan. The average Indian is slightly less wealthy than the average citizen of Cote d'Ivoire, and even if China's economy becomes the world's largest in the 2020s, as predicted by a range of economists, it will still only have a per capita wealth level close to that of the Equatorial Guinea today. At that point, India's average wealth level will be around that of Tunisia. To India and China, their 'developing' status is no slogan or diplomatic ruse. They remain acutely aware of their internal fragility and how much their viability and stability relies upon being able to steadily improve the prosperity of their people. To this mindset, other countries' nagging about 'responsible stakeholders' and the duties of great powers appears ungenerous and harsh. Beijing and New Delhi are uncomfortable with aspects of their new prominence, such as the world's attention to the contributions they are making to the problem of greenhouse gas emissions, or China's foreign exchange reserves' role in widening global financial imbalances, or the effect of the energy thirst of both on world oil prices. Their poverty and internal fragility are major reasons they have not chosen to try to play active leadership roles internationally.

As a consequence, the world still presses in uncomfortably upon China, India, Indonesia and Vietnam at a time when they feel they should be given greater voice and respect, but also as they continue to be aware of their own weaknesses. Even after the global financial crisis the dominant international voices still call for liberal democracy, neoliberal economic doctrines, individual human rights, universal action on climate change, and strict nuclear non-proliferation principles. There are many in China's elite who believe that Western fear of China's rise is the direct consequence of a shortfall in respect and recognition commensurate with its rising power. China in particular nurses a sense of historical injustice through its school curricula and even theme parks that showcase its 'century of humiliation'. Opinion polling conducted by the Lowy Institute in China in 2009 showed a markedly higher sense of grievance and demand for respect among younger Chinese than among the older generation.

But however deep their sense of grievance, the giants won't push too hard against the current international rules because, ironically, they are also the biggest beneficiaries of the way the world works. Their quiescence is for now pragmatic and accommodating, but it does not denote a meek acceptance or 'socialisation' into the current global operating rules. Behind their compliance lies an enduring sense that due acknowledgement, commensurate with their size, civilisation and history, has not been made by other countries. Respect, status and prestige are enduring objectives of these profoundly hierarchical societies. It makes even those who already occupy important formal positions, and are increasingly prominent, still highly sensitive to how others treat them, and they remain jealous of their prerogatives. Theirs is a form of national honour that European and American societies have left behind, but which eighteenth-century German philosopher Arthur Schopenhauer described thus: 'the honour of a nation consists in establishing the opinion, not only that it may be trusted (its credit), but also that it is to be feared. An attack on its rights must never be allowed to pass unheeded.'

✳

Asia's giants are a mass of contradictions. They are the greatest beneficiaries of the way the world works, but they are dissatisfied with it at the same time. They are universally acknowledged as the rising powers, but feel that the world has not yet accorded them the respect or status they deserve. Even as the older generation of people who remember foreign domination dwindles, the loss of honour and sense of humiliation is strongest among the young. Even as their pride in their achievements grows, they feel keenly every slight, and take grave offense at every perceived insult. Their border disputes with each other remain so intractable because their contested boundaries hark back to foreign domination, and any compromise conjures up memories of meek submission to foreigners. Their deepest urges to bring Europeans and Americans down to equal or even subordinate status are at the same time contradicted by the ascendancy of Western ideals of beauty, from the overwhelming use of Caucasian fashion models to the huge popularity of whitening skin creams. And the most passionately contested status competition runs internally, like a silent stream through the dealings between Asian states. Japan's and China's rivalry draws its power and intractability from deep historical currents of cultural competition. China's haughty dismissals of the significance of India's economic growth, and the ease with which Beijing can raise New Delhi's hackles come from similar sources. Asia's old rivalries of cultural derivation and independence are emerging as the twenty-first century evolves, and will affect the region's patterns of alignment and enmity as strongly as any strategic or economic forces.

Like Aurangzeb, Asian countries' experience of power has very much shaped their approach to and understanding of their own growing strength. For most of their history, their size, momentum, gravity and respect were in alignment. Prestige worked like a prevailing wind, justifying their internal systems of control, allowing invaders and foreign ideas to be absorbed and altered, protecting them from the constant warfare that afflicted early modern Europe. Then suddenly this universe was crushed by a few who wielded material, not moral force, but who gained great strength by subduing those who had once been supreme. The trauma of sudden subjugation ran deep. It could never be ignored or absorbed; it could not be reasoned away. The experience of colonialism seared into the soul of society. It is a wound that remains sensitive to the smallest slight, and one that can only be expunged by public acts of respect and contrition. The sudden shock of colonialism didn't convert Asian mindsets from hierarchical to egalitarian, it deepened the significance of material, moral and cultural hierarchies.

Despite their rhetoric about the 'democratisation of international relations', Asia's giants are still status-obsessed, and determined to regain what they see as their traditional position at the top of the ladder of international prestige and respect. This explains what foreign observers, such as Canadian political scientist Daniel Bell, find so incongruous about a Chinese cultural tendency to support the best teams rather than underdogs in sporting contests. A hierarchy of ability is to be supported, not wished against. One's status, to this mindset, is ultimately an indication of superior qualities. As their power to shape the world around them grows, this is the pattern of relationships that Asia's giants are likely to start to build in Asia and beyond. The status rivalries will be most intense with Western states and with each other. These patterns of power will shape Australia's world in the decades ahead.

5

Insular nation

Maryborough is a provincial centre of 21 000 located halfway up Australia's eastern coast. A major port for immigration and trade in the nineteenth century, the refined opulence of its public buildings is a sedate reminder that once it vied to be state capital of Queensland. Maryborough's annual agricultural show flows like a bloodline through more than a century of its history, a heartbeat that also connects it with similar festivals across Australia's rural heartland. The fashions, sideshows and rides may have evolved, but the buzz of simple enjoyment and goodwill in the bright winter sunshine returns with the caravans and stalls, year after year.

But just after 3 o'clock in the afternoon of 27 April 2005, total silence descended on the Maryborough showground. Every ride stopped, every conversation and sideshow froze, all heads tilted towards the show's loudspeakers. For the past hour, the loudspeakers had broadcast not announcements and carnival tunes but the proceedings from a courtroom in Denpasar, Indonesia. It was the same trial that was being carried live on three of the country's five free-to-air television channels and was driving record levels of internet traffic towards news websites. At Maryborough showground, shortly after Judge Linton Sirait sentenced Schapelle Lee Corby to 20 years in prison for the possession of 4.1 kilograms of marijuana at Denpasar airport in October 2004, one show-goer walked to a stall making and selling bumper stickers and commissioned one that said 'Free Schapelle'. Very soon the stall had sold out.

The pulse of outrage that greeted the sentence reverberated and built in the days and weeks that followed. A populist campaign, fanned by newspapers and talkback radio, stoked public anger and gained public advocates such as Oscar winner Russell Crowe and television host John Jarrat. Shock jocks and tabloids competed with each other to channel public bile. One talkback radio host compared the trial judges to monkeys: 'they don't even speak English. They're straight out of the trees.' Callers to talkback radio demanded Australian Special Forces be dispatched to rescue Corby. One man told a prime-time current affairs program he was prepared to face an Indonesian firing squad in exchange for her freedom. Placards appeared on highway verges proclaiming 'Free Schapelle – Boycott Bali' or even 'Fuck Bali'. A website, BanBali.com, advocating an immediate and unconditional pardon, attracted hundreds of hits. World Vision, the Red Cross, Oxfam, Caritas and Care Australia all received dozens of calls demanding a return of donations made for the relief of the victims of the 2004 Boxing Day tsunami in Indonesia. In early June, a package of white powder and a menacing letter were sent to the Indonesian embassy in Canberra, causing it to be evacuated in fear of an anthrax attack. Indonesian community leaders received abuse and death threats. Eggs were thrown at the Indonesian Consulate General in Perth.

Many were caught unawares by the scale of the response to the Corby verdict. No other Australian arrested and convicted for drug offenses overseas – not even the handful that were executed – had ever called forth such an emotional and widespread response. But what is most interesting about the episode is how it captured and conveyed some of the deep contradictions in contemporary Australian society's attitudes towards the outside world. The Corby trial and verdict underlined just how international Australian society has become. Many of Schapelle's loudest advocates relied on direct experience of having visited Bali, a trip that is made by tens of thousands of Australians each year. But the impressions they used in their arguments showed that their knowledge of Bali and Indonesia was almost non-existent. General stereotypes about corruption and incompetence were applied to the Denpasar Court with no justification or evidence – but they gained broader influence because they were based on stereotypes. Corby's plight grabbed Australians' attention because she seemed to symbolise how many felt about the outside world: a big, unpredictable, capricious place capable of suddenly turning on the small and alone. Newspaper polls found over 90 per cent of respondents believed Corby's version of events rather than the case made by the Indonesian police. This perception was met by a determination to make a difference through small acts: boycotting Bali, demanding back donations, terrorising Indonesian diplomats. Every assurance by the Australian government that such actions were ineffective or counterproductive only seemed to increase the fury and determination of Corby's supporters.

Here is the great paradox of modern Australia. Never has there been a greater gap between Australian society's enmeshment with the world and its levels of interest in the world beyond its shores. A country that is aware, as never before, that the rise of Asia holds the key to its future, for good and ill, has been steadily disinvesting in its capacity to understand and influence its regional environment. A nation that has become profoundly cosmopolitan and well-travelled over the space of two decades has, at the same time, become more belligerently self-assertive and inflexible in the face of a globalised world's challenges. When you look around at the great convergence and the coming geometries and psychology of power occurring just off Australia's northern coast, the last role you would choose to take up would be that of an insular nation. But that's exactly what we have chosen to be in the early twenty-first century.

Insular internationalists

In the two decades after 1990, Australia let in the world in greater depth, variety and volume than at any other time in its history. By the start of the century, it had lower barriers to international trade and investment than any other developed economy, whereas for most of the twentieth century it had some of the highest. Australia's trade, which had been just over a quarter of its economy in the 1960s, had grown to 42 per cent of the size of a much larger economy by 2000. The flow of investment into Australia in 2006 was twenty times as large as in 1990. By 2008 over half a million foreign students were studying at Australian schools, colleges and universities, a 20 per cent increase from the previous year and following similar increases every year for the previous decade.

By the mid-1990s over 100 000 people were migrating to Australia every year, making up over half of the country's annual population increase for the first time since the early twentieth century. The population passed 22 million at the end of September 2009: the last million was added one year faster than the previous million, and nearly two years faster than the million before that. And although Australia has always had high immigration, throughout the trans-millennial decades its immigrants were coming from a wider variety of places than ever before. Over one-quarter of Australians were born overseas, and in 1996 the number of Asian-born Australians passed one million. The number of Chinese-born citizens has increased six-fold since 1990, and the number of Indian-born has quadrupled. Two and a half million Australians speak a language other than English at home. Over one-half of all marriages in Australia each year are between people born in different countries.

The transmillennial decades also saw Australians go into the world with a confidence, frequency and impact they've never had in the past. The flow of investment out of Australia grew to 95 times its 1990 levels by 2006, with year-on-year growth in external invest-ment averaging 12 per cent between 2002 and 2007. That year the country exported twice as much capital as it imported, and Australian investment abroad equalled three-quarters of the amount of global capital invested in Australia. On any given day, there are around one million Australians living in or visiting another country. In the first six months of 2010, 6.8 million Australians – more than a quarter of the population – travelled overseas, translating into 31 interna-tional journeys per hundred Australians, compared to just 12 per one hundred in 1990. Australians' wanderlust has been increasing at an average of 11 per cent every year since 2003, now reaching the point that its numbers of short-term departures outnumber short-term arrivals by over a million a year. This has never happened before. And Australians have begun leaving on a long-term basis in ever-increasing numbers. Over the course of the transmillennial decades, long-term departures increased by on average 13 per cent each year, and Australian expats were playing ever more prominent roles in the world. A 2004 study of the Australian diaspora produced an impressive roll-call of prominent Australian expats:

In business, Australians head up McDonald's, Rio Tinto, Pizza Hut, Santos, Dow Chemical, News Corporation, Polaroid and British Airways, and hold senior executive positions in IBM, Merrill Lynch, Kellogg's, DuPont and UBS. The iconic American companies Coca-Cola and Ford were, until recently, run by Australians. The editors of the *New York Post* and *The Times* of London are Australian. The President of the World Bank was born an Australian, as was the Crown Princess of Denmark. The secretary general of the Pacific Islands Forum Secretariat is an Australian and another will soon be solicitor-general of Papua New Guinea. There are 20 Australian born and educated professors at Harvard University and the Massachusetts Institute of Technology alone. Australians and former Australians have worked in senior positions at United Nations Headquarters, in 10 Downing Street and the White House. An Australian was, until recently, Vice-Chancellor of the University of Cambridge in the UK, while another presides over the Royal Society. NASA has sent an Australian into space. Australians are prominent in Hollywood, both in front of and behind the camera, and are influential in Asia's film industry. Our success in the British arts world is just as notable: Australians run London's South Bank Centre, its Philharmonic Orchestra, its Science Museum and the Sadler's Wells Theatre. They also direct Britain's Royal Ballet School, the Royal College of Music, Edinburgh's International Film Festival, and Cardiff's Millennium Centre.

The world has always been important to Australia, but during the past two decades it has become steadily more so. A much larger proportion of its prosperity relies of global markets and investment.

More Australians work and live outside of the country than ever before. The fulcrum of world affairs has inexorably moved closer to its own shoreline. And yet during a visit to Brussels to meet Asian and European leaders in October 2010, the Australian prime minister said, 'Foreign policy is not my passion. It's not what I've spent my life doing ... I'd probably be more [comfortable] in a school watching kids learn to read in Australia than here in Brussels at international meetings.' The remark attracted little criticism or comment. Months earlier, the leader of the Opposition had also stated that international affairs was not his area of expertise. During the federal election campaign in August 2010, the world outside Australia's shores was barely mentioned. A desultory debate between the major parties' foreign affairs spokespeople attracted little attention. The two international issues that did feature in the campaign were the war in Afghanistan and the arrival of asylum seekers by boat in Australia's north-eastern waters. But a studied lack of interest in or vision about the world appeared to count little against either leader in the minds of voters.

The idea that international issues are not something that Australians care much about has been steadily growing as an accepted wisdom among the country's political class since the early 1990s. When asked about his portfolio responsibilities by two researchers in 1998, then Opposition foreign affairs spokesman Laurie Brereton began his reply with 'Well there's no votes in foreign policy'. Prime ministers who are deemed to become too enamoured with international issues are judged harshly for it. Paul Keating's perceived obsession with Asian engagement was seen to play a big role in the electorate's judgement that his pursuit of 'the big picture' had come at the expense of the concerns of ordinary Australians. John Howard told a prominent journalist during his first overseas trip as prime minister that 'Frankly I don't want to get involved in foreign policy' – despite having told another journalist a decade earlier that he would like to one day be foreign minister, and having listed foreign affairs as one of his two key areas of interest when he first entered Parliament in 1974. As prime minister, Kevin Rudd's big foreign policy initiatives and not unusually hectic international travel schedule soon earned him the sardonic nickname 'Kevin 747', and his expertise and comfort with international affairs also came to be interpreted as a lack of engagement with domestic issues. Julia Gillard and her opponent Tony Abbott would have been well aware that their statements about a lack of interest and expertise in a major element of a prime minister's job would carry little risk of damage to their popularity. Imagine the leader of an Australian political party proclaiming a lack of interest or expertise in the economy, or health, or education.

The deepening insularity of Australian society has allowed governments from both sides of politics to systematically disinvest in the primary instruments through which Australia deals with the outside world. In March 2009, detailed research by the Lowy Institute showed that Australia's budget for foreign affairs and diplomacy has progressively shrunk in real terms during the very decades that Australian society has grown more and more dependent on the outside world. By 2009, Australia had fewer diplomatic missions than every other developed country, with the exceptions of Finland, Luxembourg, New Zealand and Slovenia. Further Lowy Institute research in 2010 showed Australia's investment in international public broadcasting was just a fraction of that invested by countries it likes to compare itself to: the United States, United Kingdom, France, Germany, South Korea and Japan. Even a smaller and more secure country like the Netherlands outspends Australia in broadcasting to the rest of the world.

But even as they accepted an erosion of Australia's capacities to influence the world it was enmeshing with, the voters accepted and rewarded a dramatic investment in measures and agencies designed to keep the country 'safe' from the outside world. The message that connectivity meant vulnerability grew as a steady drumbeat during the transmillennial decades. In the years between 2000 and 2010, the budget of the Department of Defence increased by 62 per cent; that of the Australian Secret Intelligence Service by 437 per cent; that of the Office of National Assessments by 471 per cent; and that of the Australian Security Intelligence Organisation by 562 per cent. By the 2010 election, concern about terrorism had been forgotten, but hysteria about the threat from asylum seekers arriving by boat reached fever pitch. Despite just 26 000 asylum seekers arriving by boat over the past 34 years (an average of 1300 each year) both government and opposition vied with each other to throw money at the problem. In the 2010 Budget Papers the total visible pledge to addressing the asylum seekers issue is almost $654 million – a figure that does not include the substantial proportion of the Defence, Intelligence and Federal Police budgets devoted to the issue. The Opposition pledged to re-open offshore detention facilities on Nauru, a measure in itself estimated to have cost more than $1 billion between 2001 and 2007. These figures are depressing when compared to Australia's spending on its diplomacy, which is funded at just over $1 billion, or its international broadcasting budget of just $34 million; they are bizarre when they show a willingness to spend over $100 000 for each of the nearly 6000 boat-borne asylum seekers that arrived in 2010.

Pass the sunscreen

It is always risky to try to analyse the public mind, but Australia's internationalisation–insularity paradox is too stark to leave unexplained. Some commentators are dismissive, arguing that Australians are simply parochial and narrow-minded, that their opinions on international issues are invariably misguided and shouldn't be taken into account by governments formulating foreign policy.

These attitudes recall a time when diplomacy was a parlour game of aristocrats who would have been most amused at the thought that common people should have opinions on world affairs, and horrified at the thought that their opinions should count. International affairs are no longer an aristocratic pastime. Around the world people have grown steadily more aware of how much conflicts and compacts between countries can affect them as individuals, and they have developed clear opinions about how they think the world works and how it should be managed. A good case can be made that Australians' lack of interest in international affairs is a rational reaction to another widely held set of attitudes about their country and the world that have been around for a long time.

Australians can be forgiven for being more than a little cynical about the importance of the world to their daily lives. For decades they have been told that big changes are coming that will affect them profoundly. Since the 1960s, commentators have warned that the rise of Asia would challenge Australian society in profound ways. Hedley Bull, Australia's most famous and influential analyst of international affairs, wrote in 1972 about a spreading realisation that:

> The simple balance that had grown up in Asia in the 1950s
> between the communist powers and the American alliance
> system was clearly giving place to a complex balance in
> which America, Russia, China, and to an increasing extent
> Japan, were independent actors.

Bull argued that in this situation, Australia would need to accept that its security could no longer rely on its alliance with the United States, and would need to balance evenly among all of the big four. Seventeen years later, the eminent economist Ross Garnaut wrote in less foreboding terms about the economic rise of North-East Asia and its transformative effect on the world economy. This presented great opportunities for Australia, argued Garnaut, but only if its society was prepared to make a demanding and unaccustomed transition: 'the challenge of the Northeast Asian ascendancy to Australia includes the need to comprehend Northeast Asian social, economic and political institutions and languages'. For Prime Minister Paul Keating seven years later, a booming Asia challenged Australia:

> if Australia does not succeed in Asia it will not succeed anywhere. But success clearly requires more than the traditional tools of foreign policy ... our external relations can no longer exist in a separate box marked 'foreign relations' or 'foreign policy' – largely unconnected with the domestic policies which are needed to build a society which is both open and competitive and cohesive and strong.

According to Keating, to make its way in its region Australia needed to become a republic. The common thread to each of these arguments – and to dozens more in between – was that Asia was rising and Australians would have to change to avoid disaster or to make the most of it.

But Australia didn't change. Australia kept its alliance with the United States and Australians their marked comfort with Western values and societies over Asian societies. Lowy Institute polling has consistently shown Australians overwhelmingly support the alliance with the United States. They consistently feel more warmly towards Western countries – New Zealand, Canada, France, the United Kingdom and the United States – than Asian countries. Those Asian countries they do prefer are the most Westernised – Singapore and Japan. Since Garnaut's call for Asian literacy in 1989 there has been a relative decline in the numbers of Australians studying Asian languages. While Japanese is still the most widely studied foreign language and demand has surged for Mandarin Chinese, the

131

number of people studying other Asian languages is either stagnant or declining. Schools and universities have reduced their investments in the teaching of Asian languages. Nor did Australia become a republic, with close to 55 per cent of voters rejecting a 1999 referendum for an Australian head of state.

The world did not punish Australians for their obduracy. Even as the alliance with the United States strengthened, no destabilising competition with China or Russia threatened its shores. The nuclear attack that many had warned would come due to Australia hosting American communication bases never eventuated. The Koreans and Japanese, soon to be joined by the Chinese and the Indians, continued to buy Australia's resources and visit its resorts. The economy boomed, and Australians became more wealthy than ever despite their lack of interest in the cultures, histories or languages of the people they were trading with. Far from being shut out of the region, Australia participated in the founding of regional organisations in spite of retaining Queen Elizabeth II as its formal head of state.

Indeed, practically every international issue that really worried Australians at some stage over the past 60 years has seemed to simply fade away without even a whimper. Their major fears after World War II were over a resurgent Japanese militarism and the creeping tide of communism. But Japan turned out to be the most benign of great powers, adopting a stance of extreme pacifism and being consistently – and almost unbelievably – reasonable whenever provoked. Instead of a threat, Japan became Australia's closest partner in Asia, collaborating with Canberra in the founding of a range of regional bodies. While the communist menace lasted longer, by the end of the 1970s it also was a waning force. Beijing had coupled its market reform with a strictly pragmatic and non-provocative attitude to its international affairs; Vietnam had become embroiled in a bitter war in Cambodia; and the Soviet Union, China and Vietnam seemed more intent on fighting among themselves than in spreading world revolution. Australia's strategic experts got the jitters about the Soviet navy in the Pacific and Indian Oceans and the Russian invasion of Afghanistan from time to time, but the rest of the population paid it little attention. By the end of the 1980s the 'red menace' had sunk into the sands of irrelevance.

Nor did the United States succumb to the isolationism that many feared would follow its defeat in the Vietnam War, leading it to pack up its alliances and go home. These fears flickered again in the mid-1980s when New Zealand's no-nuclear ships policy led to its expulsion from the ANZUS alliance, and then again briefly in the early 1990s, when Thailand stepped away from its alliance with the United States and the Philippines closed American bases at Subic Bay and Clark Field. Another set of jitters came when serious trade tensions began to surface between Japan and the United States at the end of the 1980s. But through all of these setbacks, the United States stayed engaged on Australia's side of the Pacific Ocean. The rise of China and the War on Terror brought America's role back to centre stage, as existing allies strengthened commitments, former allies renewed commitments, and never allies and former enemies forged new commitments. By 2010 the demand for a sustained American presence in the Indo-Pacific was greater than at any time since the mid-1960s.

Another deep and even older fear that many Australians still held was that crowded, poor Asian countries would suddenly discover their resource-rich, sparsely populated country and invade in great numbers. Concerns were particularly deep about the big societies in Asia – Indonesia, China and India. But while ingrained insecurities about the vulnerability of Australia to a flood of poor Asians remains and animates the hysteria over boat-borne asylum seekers, perceptions of Asian societies as crowded and poor have been eroded by a growing awareness of the Asian economic miracle. Stereotypes of East Asians could not but change in the face of such factors as the large inflows of well-heeled tourists arriving and underpinning a booming sector of the economy, the growing number of Australians aware that their country's (and their own) economic good fortune is based on rapid development in Asia, and the obvious wealth of Asian migrants and students. Despite the recent outburst of xenophobia that described the arc of Pauline Hanson's political career, the visceral discomfort of most Australians with the influx of Asian immigrants has largely been on the wane. Australia's non-discriminatory immigration policy has not resulted in the country being 'swamped by Asians' as Hanson predicted.

Another concern, though mostly confined to the policy wonks, was that Australia would be shut out of the markets on which it had become so dependent by the rise of a closed-shop Asian region-alism. In the early 1990s – as Americans began to worry about their trade imbalance with Japan; as the Asian tigers strode from quarter to booming quarter of growth; and as Americans and Euro-peans crowed about the superiority of their democracy, liberty and capitalism – leaders and public intellectuals in Asia began to push back. The economic success of Asian countries, the most rapid and sustained development the world had ever seen, was a direct consequence of the way Asian societies and political systems were organised, they argued. It was 'Asian values' that mandated the political, economic and social structures that Westerners criticised as authoritarian, economically distorting and patronising. 'Asian values' brought the stability, discipline and teamwork underpinning the Asian economic miracle. The more conspiratorially minded, such as Malaysian Prime Minister Mahathir, warned that Western criticisms ultimately sought to dilute Asia values and thereby under-mine Asian countries' challenge to the West's global economic dominance. Only by coming together in an exclusive economic bloc could the Asian tigers protect their political and economic systems, achieve compound gains from each other's dynamism, and project a greater Asian voice into global economic institutions. It was this view of Asia that motivated Mahathir to try to block Australia's access to Asian regional bodies. It was a fear that he would succeed that led Australian governments into a decade of ungainly contortions in their Asian diplomacy.

But yet again, the threat just disappeared. All of Asia's regional bodies failed to produce what they had been set up to achieve, and as they lost momentum they succumbed to bright shirts and bland communiqués. With neither global nor Asian trade talks able to deliver freer flows of goods and investment, Asian countries began to pair off and sign economic agreements together. By April 2001, Australia was drawn into this dynamic by that most energetic dealmaker, Singapore. More followed, as Australia signed deals with Thailand, the United States, and Chile; and others remain under negotiation – with China, Japan, Korea, Malaysia, the Gulf countries, the Association of South-East Asian Nations, and the South Pacific countries. Australia is now more deeply and dynamically linked to its key markets by a tapestry of special deals than ever before. Mahathir is long gone, and no Asian leader could hope to argue for an exclusive bloc that suddenly cuts all of these meticulously negotiated trade deals.

In hindsight, the world has appeared to become more benign with each passing year. All of Australia's disputes with its neighbours – over East Timor, tourist advisories, the jailing of Australian businessmen and drug couriers, bashed students, standing up for whales – seem to just blow over despite the dire warnings of foreign policy experts. Nielsen global polling has found Australians' levels of economic optimism among the highest in the world, surrounded as they are by the societies of booming Asia. Meanwhile Americans, Japanese, and Europeans plumb the depths of economic pessimism. Nothing from the outside world seems to have worsened the safety, health or wealth of Australians. They can go pretty much wherever they want on Earth, and get pretty much whatever they want. Worrying about the outside world is too much like hard work.

The double disincentive

Australians are not naive enough to believe that the entire world is benign. When disaster hits some corner of the globe, they watch in horror and fascination as much as any society does. The Boxing Day tsunami in the Indian Ocean, which saw Australians donate $240 million to help the victims, shows how engaged and concerned Australians can be when other people are in need or distress. But to the great majority of Australians, war, pestilence and collapse are things that happen to other people, a long way away. The Australian psyche has remoteness embedded deeply in its operating system, despite the fact that 95 per cent of its people live in increasingly globalised and cosmopolitan cities. The original perception of isolation from the British Isles has never left, even as Britain has become less and less important to Australia, and the closer countries of Asia have become ever more central to its fortunes and well-being. Living in one of the only countries on Earth that shares no land borders with another, Australians are accustomed to peering out over vast oceans when they want to see what other societies are doing. And so when danger or catastrophe are really quite close – as they have been over the past decade, in East Timor, Aceh, Solomon Islands, Fiji, Thailand and Papua New Guinea – they seem as distant as if they had occurred in Africa or Europe or South America. It is a perception of remoteness that can be rather comforting at times; bad things might happen to the rest of the world but Australia is too far away to be affected.

To go with their remoteness, Australians also seem to be all-too conscious of their limited size among nations. No other country seems so intent on 'punching above its weight' or measuring its achievements against those of other societies on a per capita basis. It is a perception that has long troubled the country's strategic thinkers, who for well over a century have advocated much higher immigration levels to allow the country to defend itself against the much more populous countries in its region. As far back as 1938 the eminent economist Sir John Crawford observed morosely, 'Australia seems to provoke more interest as a possible prize than as a future great power'. Seven years later, Foreign Minister Herb Evatt fought hard to include in the United Nations Charter a clause that would protect smaller nations when the powerful wanted to use the UN to interfere in their domestic affairs. Even now, Australians are content to commit their own armed forces to overseas operations in much smaller numbers than those of countries with smaller economies and populations. The great luxury of having a superpower ally is that you can permanently fill niche roles.

This is the double disincentive that helps to suck the public's interest out of world affairs: Australia is too far away to be affected, and too small to make a difference. It is a strong undercurrent that, paradoxically, seems to become stronger as the world becomes more complex and immediate. Social researcher Hugh Mackay argues that Australians have become more insular in recent decades as they see their lives prey to powerful forces that shape their fortunes but are beyond their control. Their disengagement reflects not lack of interest or concern, but a sense of powerlessness: 'the happiest people', he reported, 'were those whose horizons were most limited, whose concerns were unremittingly local, immediate and personal'.

Such feelings of powerlessness could only have been increased among those supporters of Schapelle Corby who, having printed bumper stickers and posters, urged Bali boycotts and collected signatures, finally realised that what they did would have no effect. Mackay notes also a shift away from serious current affairs in the Australian media and the rise of lifestyle and reality programs. A growing sense of powerlessness has led to a hedonistic determination just to enjoy life:

> Australians are ready to leave politics to the politicians,
> economics to the economists and international relations to
> the diplomats. They want to disengage from the national
> agenda so they can get on with having a good life in the best,
> safest country on earth.

Come in spinner

It's not that Australians have never been endangered by the world beyond their shores. They have. And it's not that they've forgotten. They haven't. Memories of the shock of hearing about the fall of Singapore, or of Saigon, lie deep within the national consciousness. But these aren't the painful, searing memories that are held by most other people on Earth – and by Indigenous Australians – of foreign troops marching down their capital's broad boulevards, of being bullied and humiliated by invaders, of national symbols defaced, of living frugally while a government pays off huge war debts or reparations. Immigrants to Australia are often astounded at how benign are the supposed demons that stalk their new nation's subconsciousness.

The reason is that the real crisis always seems to be averted before it reaches Australia. It seems that the country has a cosmic panic button that brings someone or something to its salvation when things are starting to look ugly. The greatest threat the country has faced came in 1942, when the Japanese Imperial Army swept through South-East Asia, captured the 'impregnable' base of Singapore and reached Timor, New Guinea and Solomon Islands. Many of Australia's best troops were fighting a desperate campaign against German and Italian forces in North Africa. Japanese planes bombed Darwin, Broome and other northern Australian cities, and Japanese submarines infiltrated Sydney Harbour. In these desperate straits the arrival of United States forces could not have come at a more welcome juncture. The American navy blunted the Japanese advance with the battle for the Coral Sea and the desperate fighting on Guadalcanal. United States forces based themselves in Brisbane, and with Australian, New Zealand, British and Indian troops began to push the Japanese out of South-East Asia.

Twenty years later, it was the Japanese who came to the rescue. Since European colonisation, Australia had been closely tied into a system of increasingly exclusive imperial trade. Australian meat, wool and dairy goods fed generations of Britons, who in return supplied Australia with cloth and manufactures, immigrants and investment. Whitehall used its trading deals with its colonies and dominions, codified in the Ottawa Agreements of 1932, to lock rising industrial challengers such as Japan out of crucial markets they needed to further develop their industries. Canberra clung to these agreements into the 1950s, even though they made little sense in light of its trading potential, and though they were highly distorting to its economic development. It came as a great shock, then, when in 1961 Britain announced it was applying to join the European Economic Community – a move that would sever its obligations to buy from its former empire in favour of ever closer trading linkages with continental Europe. By 1971, when Britain finally joined Europe, Australia could have found itself in the same position that Vietnam or Cuba did when the Soviet Union collapsed. (Deprived of assured markets, aid and investments, both countries fell into economic crisis: Vietnam underwent painful reforms and boomed; Cuba continues to decline.) But by the early 1960s, the Japanese economy had been rebuilt to a level that saw it become a strong importer of food, wool, energy and minerals – from Australia. One resource- and space-constrained set of islands had replaced another in a relationship of the most perfect complementarity with the Australian economy.

The next lucky break occurred long before Australians even knew they were in trouble. In March 1966 an experimental drilling rig found oil in the Marlin field in Bass Strait. The backers of the project, ESSO and BHP, pressed ahead with further prospecting and by 1968 had found the huge Kingfish and Halibut oil fields, thought to have a capacity of 1.5 billion barrels of oil. By 6 October 1973, when Egyptian tanks crossed the Suez Canal in force, Bass Strait was yielding 300 000 barrels of oil every day. When Arab oil producing countries embargoed supplies to countries they believed supported Israel, many powerful and comfortable societies soon realised their vulnerability. In the United States, long queues formed at gas stations and scuffles broke out. With the oil price quadrupling, rationing was implemented, and Americans were asked to forgo Christmas lights. In Britain the embargo precipitated an energy crisis amidst a 'winter of discontent' that brought down a government. Along with Germany, Switzerland and Norway, Britain banned flying, driving and boating on weekends. Sweden rationed kerosene and heating oil and the British prime minister appealed to Britons to heat only one room. The Netherlands imposed prison sentences on those found using more than their allocation of electricity. Australians barely noticed. Petrol prices rose a bit, but not enough to worry anyone. There was greater excitement when the Queen opened the Sydney Opera House and Australia won the Federation Cup. The biggest controversy in Australia was over a painting titled 'Blue Poles', purchased for the National Gallery at great cost. Or over the biggest film of the year, 'Alvin Purple', a soft-porn comedy about a man to whom women are irresistibly attracted. Australia even benefited from the oil crisis, for one country that most deeply felt its oil vulnerability was Japan, and with characteristic single-mindedness Tokyo embarked on a program of energy efficiency and diversity of fuel sources and supply. The result was a big boost for Australia's coal exports and the emergence of a major buyer for its uranium.

In September 1999, Australia was brought face-to-face with its lack of leverage in an unpredictable region. As militiamen rampaged through East Timor after its vote to separate from Indonesia, and thousands of Australians marched to demand the government do something to stop the carnage, Canberra could only look at the wreckage of its relationship with its northern neighbour. To insert Australian troops without Jakarta's agreement would have been an act of war and almost certainly resisted. But none of the government's calls were being taken. Indonesians regarded Australia as the author of East Timor's impending separation, and the thought of foreign troops on Indonesian soil was anathema. Once again, Canberra was able to rely on American help at the last minute. President Clinton played a strong role in supporting Australia's efforts to co-ordinate a regional peace-keeping mission at the September 1999 APEC meeting in Wellington, and he later pressured Indonesia to either end the violence or accept peace-keepers. US Secretary of Defense William Cohen flew to Indonesia to warn that there would be 'economic consequences' if Indonesia did not 'make the right choice' in East Timor. By late September, the first Australian troops of the international peace-keeping force arrived on the island. Indonesian forces withdrew. Not a shot was fired.

Any person who had led such a charmed life could not fail to have been shaped by the experience. The repeated intervention of someone or something to avert harm would lead a person to stop worrying about the challenges of the future and become unfailingly optimistic. Thinking about risks or accidents would be a waste of time. The same has happened to Australia. A country which has always relied on a strong ally for protection, which has always been saved from calamities by sudden interventions, will never be good at thinking hard about the risks it faces and how it can protect itself.

Australian thinking and policy-making about international affairs suffers from a culture of serendipity, which erodes its ability for long-term thinking and to make tough choices. Foreign affairs becomes a question of managing a web of relationships, and all too often when a problem is foreseen the easy solution is to set up an institution, coalition or meeting to resolve it. Institutions – whether regional, global or issues-based – have become the band-aids of Australian foreign policy, prescribed for any and all ailments and to cauterise the need for any further hard thinking about the issue and its implications. So for example APEC was the answer to preventing USA–Japan trade tensions destroying the Asia Pacific economic dynamic: little thought was given in Canberra to the long-running causes of friction between East Asia's booming economies and the United States which still exist today as APEC enters its twenty-second year.

Furious agreement

As every news editor knows, it is controversy and disagreement that attracts attention: if it bleeds, it leads. Any issue that has important people denouncing, dissenting or denigrating each other will make the front pages and lead the news broadcasts. Debate, angst and sudden swings in political fortune – all covered gleefully by the media – have accompanied the extraordinary changes in Australian society and governance over the past 60 years. Australian trade policy today would be unrecognisable to those who designed and operated it just after World War II. The ethnic diversity of Australia's cities would horrify those who ran immigration policy in the1950s. Australia's currency, national anthem, holidays and honours were all replaced in the 1960s and 1970s. Economic policy changed fundamentally: a floating dollar, an independent Reserve Bank, low tariffs, and deregulated labour markets and financial sectors. Laws relating to women's right to work are now part of the furniture. University education has become broadly accessible and was at one time free; now it's subject to elaborate cost sharing. Universal free health care has come, and gone. Aboriginal Australians are now citizens. Great Australian icons – Qantas, the Commonwealth Bank, Australia Telecom – are no longer owned and run by the government.

Amid all this change, it's hard to believe that one area of national policy is much the same as it was in the 1950s. But in foreign policy, the relationships, techniques and methods that Australia uses today are remarkably similar to those it used before the television age. The cornerstone of its entire foreign and strategic policy is its alliance with the United States, signed in September 1951. It is no longer a three-way alliance – after the US froze out New Zealand in 1986 – but its founding document and day-to-day management are unchanged. So are the basic structures of the intelligence-sharing agreement Australia joined with the United States and United Kingdom in 1948, an arrangement that makes its relationship with the other English-speaking countries more intimate than with any other country. In 1944–45 Australia was a founding member of the United Nations, the World Bank, the International Monetary Fund, and these same global institutions, along with the more recent World Trade Organization, remain vital contexts for Australian diplomacy. Relationships with neighbouring countries, other than New Zealand, still have to be managed in a manner appropriate to challenging but essential relationships. Australia's diplomats still present credentials, make representations and send cables back to headquarters. The regional organisations that Australia has joined are of a more recent vintage, but it's hard to argue that much of the heavy lifting of its foreign relations is done through these bodies.

Nor has there been much controversy or disagreement between the major parties about the substance or methods of Australian foreign policies. Disagreements have happened – over the Vietnam War, the recognition of Communist China, Indonesia's annexation of East Timor – but never in a way that threatens the basic common-sense positions that both sides of politics hold about Australia's international affairs. Even while denouncing each other, the Labor and Liberal Parties have never advocated leaving the alliance with America, or replacing free trade with either complete self-sufficiency or some sort of exclusive economic bloc, or that there is no longer a useful role for the United States in keeping things stable in the Western Pacific. Broad evolutions of Australia's foreign policy – such as strong advocacy of nuclear non-proliferation, or support for regional organisations, or the negotiation of preferential trade deals – have generally seen whoever happened to be in opposition follow the government line, make some occasional cosmetic criticism, and then continue the same policies once in office.

Perhaps the biggest divergence between the parties came in the mid-1990s, when a conservative government moved away from a decades-long tradition of conducting foreign policy. For much of Australia's post-war history, government of both sides of politics had championed international organisations, whether global, regional or issue-based, as the best place for a small, remote country to protect its interests. On coming to office in March 1996, the Howard government was more sceptical of the value of international organisations, and adopted a much more pragmatic, bilateral, interests-based approach to stewarding Australia's international interests. Yet none but the foreign affairs club noticed. Apart from the odd dismissive comment, the Howard government maintained Australia's support for international organisations. It even made use of them when it needed to. And none of the other basic settings of Australia's relations with the world were disturbed.

Of course there have been people from within Australian society who have strongly criticised the central tenets of the country's foreign policy. Almost from its inception in September 1951, some Australians have argued for the repudiation of the American alliance.

Critics charge the alliance with a range of offences: it drags Australia into America's wars and makes it guilty by association for all of the atrocities done in the name of the American empire; by hosting United States listening bases on Australian soil, a country that should be remote from a nuclear exchange among the great powers becomes a primary target of attack; by associating with George W Bush's 'civilizational' War on Terror, Australia has increased its own profile as a priority target for jihadist terrorist attack; by tying itself to American interests in the Pacific, Australia cuts itself off from developing intimate and lasting relationships with its Pacific neighbours.

Another strong line of critique has been directed towards Canberra's development of close working relationships with undemocratic governments in Asia: by coddling dictators like Indonesia's President Suharto, Australian governments cheapen the quality of democracy and liberty within Australia; by treating soft authoritarian Singapore as a normal state, Australia in effect endorses paternalistic, illiberal government elsewhere in the world; by treating the 'butchers of Beijing' with respect and even deference, Australian governments are showing that the country's foreign policy stands for nothing but tawdry economic gain. And then there are the advocates of an extreme makeover in Australia's foreign relations: Australia should abandon its adolescent dependence on the United States on the one hand, and its pragmatic, interests-based regional relations on the other, and fully embrace an Asian future. Whether this means a regional association or just deeper engagement, it cannot be done in a half-hearted way, and must be embarked upon without reservations.

These critiques have been around for a long time and have become familiar call-and-response routines played out on op-ed pages and talk shows. But they have never congealed into a serious division between the major parties or into genuinely viable alternatives to the current policy settings. They have never become genuine and deep divisions in the electorate over the direction of the country's foreign relations. Opinion polling shows that despite these debates, over 80 per cent of Australians support the alliance with the United States. Over 70 per cent believe China is important to Australia's economic future. People are evenly divided on the wisdom of the war in Afghanistan. There is strong support for Australia's involvement in global and regional associations. Australians are remarkably optimistic about their country's future in the world, which they see as largely a benign place. There is an almost even three-way split between those who think Australia is part of Asia, those who think it is part of the Pacific, and those who don't think it's part of any region. With so much other colour and movement, debate and intrigue in Australian public life, it's little wonder that so little of the national headspace is reserved for thinking about the rest of the world.

*

Few Australians would argue that what happens in the world has little relevance for Australia. To the contrary, most would agree that the world has been very good for their country. It has been a much needed source of markets and investment, a provider of cars and electronics, and generally welcoming and safe for those Australians who holiday or study overseas. Indeed, the world seems to suit Australia better and better with each passing year. Those issues Australians used to worry about have either been washed away by the current of history, or were suddenly forestalled by the dependable hand of luck. Much of this has been achieved without any attempt by Australia to shape the world around it – which is just as well, because it's too far away and too small to make much of a difference. And the settings of Australia's foreign policy seem to have worked so well that it's one of the only policy areas on which the major parties don't disagree. But if history tells us anything, it's that nothing is as vulnerable as an inexorable trend.

6

Here comes the world

Poets and song-writers like to describe time as a river that flows steadily, inexorably between future, present and past. Time moved to the regular alternation of the monsoon winds for the traders who sailed their dhows along the coasts of Arabia, India and South-East Asia until the sixteenth century. For centuries the monsoon winds brought and took Arab, Indian, Malay and Chinese trade boats along the great arced coastline of Asia, in an out of its great ports: Hangzhou, Guangzhou, Malacca, Calicut, Cambay,

Hormuz, Aden. No single kingdom tried to dominate or control the trade. Ships from China, Sumatra, Gujarat, Malabar and Arabia respected each other's right to passage – and regularly carried goods and passengers for each other. Time for the Aztecs was the steady drum beat of the calendar of religious festivals that set the rhythm of sowing seed, irrigation, harvesting and marketing. The lucky ones would experience the Xiuhmolpilli ceremony, held every 52 years to restart the calendar of rituals and agriculture. To lose the steady rhythm of ceremony would be to be out of kilter with the cosmic cycles of the sun, moon and Venus, and to risk being deserted by Tlaloc, the rain god.

But time isn't a steady flowing river. It's much more like a record player with a loose drive belt that will play a record very slowly for a while before suddenly speeding up and playing the music too fast. And just as there's no way to predict when a record player's worn out belt will slip or stick, it's almost impossible to tell when history is about to lurch forwards.

The traders and farmers in fourteenth-century Arabia and Meso-america were unaware that the third son of King John of Portugal had used his considerable wealth to rebuild and repopulate a village called Terçanabal, which he renamed Vila do Infante. Henry the Navigator had become fascinated by the trade the Arabs plied across northern Africa, and was determined that the fortunes of Portugal's Aviz dynasty would be made in this vast continent. The answer was to dominate Africa's north-western coast, eventually joining forces with the legendary Prester John, a Christian king who was said to live in central Africa. The problem was that European ships weren't able to handle the distances, strong winds, shoals and ocean currents of Africa's Atlantic coasts. Since the time of the Romans, Europe's shipping had been confined to galleys that hugged the coastline, relying on familiar landmarks and historical charts for navigation. But at Vila do Infante, Henry sponsored a naval program

that experimented with the known shipbuilding and sailing technologies of the time.

Henry's engineers combined three technologies to develop a ship
as revolutionary to the fifteenth century as the atom bomb was to the
twentieth. The first was the lateen rig, a triangular sail attached to
the mast along the line of the keel which allowed a ship to tack into
the wind for sustained periods. The second was the carvel method
of hull construction that produced a ship that was bigger and
stronger and could move through the water with greater speed and
agility. The third was the ephemeris, a detailed matrix that allowed
the calculation of a ship's latitude on the open sea. The result was
the carrack, a large ocean-going ship that was stable in high seas,
could tack into the wind and move quickly before the wind, and
was highly manoeuvrable and able to sail over shoals thanks to its
shallow draft. And its captains could sail confidently southwards,
calculating their latitude all the way. It was on the carrack *Santa
Maria* that Christopher Columbus sailed westwards towards the
Americas in 1492. Another carrack, *Sao Gabriel*, carried Vasco da
Gama past the Cape of Good Hope and on to India in 1497. Between
the 1440s – when Henry's engineers cracked the secret of the carrack – and 1500, history had sped up, and was soon to bring the
gentle rhythms of Asia's trading dhows and Mesoamerica's festivals
to a close. The Spanish brought Mesoamerica's cosmic festivals to an
end just as brutally as the Portuguese imposed control on the Indo-
Pacific trading system that had never been controlled by anyone, and
then pitilessly exploited it.

Time's sudden lurches forward happened before and since Henry
the Navigator became interested in Africa. Seemingly innocuous
developments that emerge over quite short periods have led to major
reconfigurations of the world. A sudden surge in the birth rate of
the barbarian tribes of northern Europe led to the fall of the Roman
Empire. Or the panicked but disciplined response of some shoguns

and their society that ultimately led to the dismantling of colonialism around the globe. Or the experiments with a decentralised form of communications by some American Defense Department engineers that leads to ... a dramatic shift back to a world in which societies' proportions of the world's population is about the same as their contribution to global economic activity.

This concluding chapter argues that it's more likely than not that we will look back on the transmillennial decades as a period when time lurched forward. It argues that it is more likely than not that the steep growth in wealth and power of Asia's giants will disrupt the familiar rhythms of Australia's dealings with the world, just as the invention of the carrack disrupted the centuries-long rhythms of the Asian traders and the Aztec farmers.

Megasize me

India and China each has a larger population than any of the earth's continents, other than the one they occupy. China's population is a bit smaller than Africa's and South America's put together; India's nearly adds up to Europe's plus the Middle East's. Whatever happens to them in the decades ahead, the chances that what happened in both of the giants during the transmillennial decades will *not* profoundly reshape the world of the twenty-first century are very small. If they continue to grow at around their current rates, the global economy will re-center on them. Even if they suddenly stop growing at these rates and lapse back to their pre-boom momentum, they will continue to be major economies whose consumption still drags the global economy this way and that. If their detractors are right, and they are headed for a major economic and social meltdown, the fall-out from their collapse will define the rest of the century. All of this holds irrespective of what happens in the rest of the world. The United States may be headed for a renewed spurt of innovation-led growth, similar to what happened in the early 1990s. Europe may leave its doldrums behind and find new sources of dynamism. Japan may as well. But none of this will change the fact that China and India have arrived as major shapers of how the world works, and their preferences, enthusiasms and aversions will have a strong effect on the choices that other societies face.

The giants' economic growth does not automatically translate into all-round influence, but it is a lead indicator of other proficiencies and dynamics. As the Indian economy grows, the spending power of its people increases. Their expectations rise and they demand to be able to consume more of a greater variety of the things that make life enjoyable. As the Chinese economy expands by one-tenth each passing year, it accumulates more and more money that it can invest with transformative effect both at home and in other countries. As China tries to keep pace with the runaway growth in its electricity needs – by building a new power station each week – it can't help but become the world's leader in power station design and innovation. Never mind its low number of Nobel laureates: any other country that wants to install cutting-edge technology, from nuclear power plants to high-speed trains, can't afford to ignore what China has on offer. As they grow wealthier, Indians' sense of entitlement isn't limited to their own consumption – it extends to what they see as their country's fair dues. China's ambitions grow as its willingness to compromise over them falls, and it begins to invest more money in better missiles, ships, tanks and submarines. As it starts to compare its capabilities with the world's leading powers, it also begins to invest in the quality, doctrine and training of its men in uniform.

But even without focusing on these other coming strengths, the sheer size and growth rates of the Chinese and Indian economies mean that they will be the key shapers of globalisation in the twenty-first century. Their decisions on tariffs, standards and currencies will sculpt the size, course and shape of the arteries of world trade and finance in the decades ahead. Whether or not they buttress their economic preferences with formal agreements and frameworks will depend on how much each of the giants can free itself from the concerns of its internal stability, and agree with the other major centres of economic heft on a common vision for the global economy.

Their exact preferences for the world economy are hard to predict and will probably evolve as their societies and the world around them changes, but some preoccupations are likely to endure. The greatest preoccupation for each, for the foreseeable future, will be their acute sensitivity to their dependence on the outside world for the oxygen of their development and stability: energy, minerals and food. The choices that each of the giants make will shape the options for all other countries involved in the trade in these basic ingredients of economic health.

A related worry will be the signs of volatility in the global economy, particularly as investment courses around the globe in greater volume and with greater velocity. Each of the giants, joined by other big countries such as Indonesia, is acutely aware of its own internal fragility; the multiple tension and fracture points in societies where the aspirations and differences of hundreds of millions constantly rub against each other. The last thing any of the big emerging economies needs is a global economy that can suddenly deaden growth rates, or squeeze energy flows, or throw millions out of work. A constant awareness of their vulnerabilities will provide a constant temptation for China, India, Indonesia and the other big Asian economies to try to intervene in markets to smooth out volatility and reduce uncertainty. Whether and how they do will have major effects on the pace and shape of globalisation.

Their preoccupations will not only be shaped by their vulnerabilities. The giants' growing sense of their centrality to the world economy will make some of their demands more insistent. As they gain size, India, China, Indonesia, Vietnam and others will start to demand a formal voice in any and all global economic talks commensurate with their size and importance. Whether they match their voice with a positive vision of what they want to achieve depends on how much headspace they have left after worrying about their vulnerabilities, and whether this vision is compatible with the expectations of the other centres of power will determine the fate of global trade and investment rules during this century. Another constant irritation will be any frameworks of global property rights that reflect an era of Euro-American domination and Asian weakness and exclusion. Wherever big Western mining companies have sewn up 'tier one' resource deposits, the Asian giants will be determined to break that monopoly as much from the need to erase contemporary reminders of their age of exclusion as from the need to ensure resource security and the diversification of supply of key minerals. They will also be predisposed, when their own interests aren't directly affected, to take the side of other former colonies and developing countries in their disputes with Western countries. Ultimately, a strong motivation for their actions will be the giants' rivalries with each other for access, supplies, markets and deals. As inclination twins with sheer size, in the decades ahead Asia's continental economies will shape the global economy into which Australia trades and invests in much greater scale and impact than currently.

The trouble with strength

Asia's rising giants have never had this sort of power in the modern, global context before. Their new ability to influence the world around them asks uncomfortable questions about what they want to achieve. It sets up expectations among their own people, and apprehensions in other societies. Of course, Asia's big countries have always been aware of their size and history. They have had the ability to coerce and the capacity to buy compliance from among the small states that surround them for decades. They have been willing to use their size and strength close to home, usually for defensive or emotive causes. But their use of force has mostly been clumsy; rarely has it been decisive. It has nearly always come at great cost, both in lives and resources and the perceptions of others. Whenever China, India, Indonesia or Vietnam have resorted to force to resolve an issue, they have increased the misgivings of their smaller neighbours. And for all of their preponderance close to home, Asia's giants have always been aware of their vulnerability to the forceful intervention of powerful countries located beyond their immediate neighbourhood.

As they grow, the giants are starting to have influence beyond their immediate surrounds. The arrival of this status has occurred over the past decade, and has been completely unexpected. Their gravitational power is the lead indicator. India's and China's growing appetite for energy, minerals and food have taken the global markets for these commodities by surprise. Supply has been tight due to decades of underinvestment in production, and the close correlation of price rises with the giants' demand increases has drawn attention to their impact on global commodity markets. Awareness of their effects on global inflation, unemployment in the developed world, and greenhouse gas emissions has followed closely behind.

Despite long wanting to be recognised as leading powers, China and India are not particularly comfortable with all of this attention. It's nice to be admired as 'I Did It My Way' success stories, but the new great power status that is conferred upon them from far and wide sits uncomfortably with their ongoing self-perceptions as poor countries still struggling in a world set up to rich countries' preferences. Nor does either country quite understand this gravitational form of power. On the upside, it would be nice to be able to leverage all of this acknowledgement and attention to get greater access to markets and key commodities, to begin to reshape elements of world affairs that seem biased against them, and to elicit the appropriate amounts of respect. To some extent, China is long practised at doing this. During its imperial era, it was able to leverage other societies' desire to trade with China to compel them to pay tribute to the emperor. Even during the modern era, it has been able to maintain its diplomatic isolation of Taiwan by premising any and all positive relations with China on other countries' adherence to the one-China principle. But beyond this, China seems unsure about how to wield its gravitational power for positive ends. It often leads to considerable frustration that, amidst all of the attention and acknowledgement, China is treated suspiciously and often denied what it asks for.

Even more perplexing for the giants is their uncertainty about how to manage the downsides of their gravitational influence, particularly when it sets up expectations and demands from other countries that could influence their own choices about their economies and societies. Gravitational power has had some effect on their position within international agencies, particularly as admiration of their successes has led some countries to be more sympathetic to their positions. But ultimately the giants remain awkward and defensive in international negotiations. They are unconvinced of global or regional agencies' capacity to bring about real change, and wary of their ability to connect opponents into common fronts. By and large the existing institutions and rules that regulate how the world works are good for India, China, Indonesia and other rising Asian countries, and none are yet convinced that their efforts to alter the things that irk them can succeed without damaging the largely positive situation that exists at present.

With economic growth will come much more formidable military capabilities and financial clout. The Asian giants already have huge military forces: China has 2.25 million men on active duty; India has 1.3 million; Vietnam just under half a million. All are increasing their military budgets by between 2 and 3 per cent each year, and investing heavily in cutting-edge, high-technology equipment, weapons and military doctrine. Even though they may trail their main adversaries in terms of their sheer capacity to do harm, China and India have not tried to match those ahead of them across the spectrum. Rather, they have concentrated on building weapons systems and capabilities that can target their likely opponents' greatest weaknesses. China knows that in any serious conflict it is likely going to have to square off against the United States. The greatest vulnerability of American forces is that they will need to operate on the other side of the Pacific Ocean from the continental United States. China's People's Liberation Army has therefore focused on building capabilities to attack advanced naval forces and supply and communications lines. India's main strategic competitor is China, which depends heavily on energy imports that have to traverse the Indian Ocean between the Gulf and China. New Delhi knows that by investing in state-of-the-art naval capabilities it can substantially even the arm-wrestle with Beijing. These military capabilities need never be used to decisively shape how the world works, and the deepening dependence of all of the players in the Asian power dynamic on a functioning international economy means that the decision to use force in a way that could escalate would likely have costs many times greater than what it could achieve. But even if using coercion has become less likely, the capacity or inability to command certain outcomes at acceptable cost forms a background framework, or skeleton, that determines how other forms of power can be used and for what purposes.

Overlaying the military map will be a distinctive map of financial and economic power. Depending on how quickly China liberalises its capital markets and currency exchange rules, Shanghai will become a global financial centre rivalling the roles London and New York played during the twentieth century. China's industrial and services sectors will move even further to the heart of the global economy, and will gradually reshape the Asian region's economies towards near-total complementarity. Mumbai may well emerge as a substantial financial centre as well, perhaps playing a role akin to that played by Frankfurt today, and India will also become a centre of services and manufacturing dynamism. Both countries are likely to be major consumption engines for the world economy. The opportunities this will give China, and to a lesser extent India, to exert influence over regional countries that need to access their consumers, factories, consultants, call centres, capital markets and currency swaps, will be substantial. Asia's configuration of military, economic and financial might is changing inexorably, and will structure the terrain over which this region's international affairs play out.

But by no means does this imply that China and India will, at some stage in the twenty-first century, establish some sort of joint condominium over Asia, in which all other countries willingly accept their leadership and assent to their bidding. Nor does it suggest a bipolar future for Asia, as the smaller countries gravitate to one or other of the giants, or to China versus the United States. A closer look at the existing, and almost certainly enduring, patterns of rivalry and suspicion suggest a much more complex set of alignments and relationships will develop in Asia in the future.

The first dynamic to keep in mind is that none of the giants is trusted by the smaller countries that surround it. China has fought wars with many of its neighbours: Japan, South Korea, India, Russia and Vietnam, and in living memory was supporting communist insurgencies in a series of countries in South-East Asia. It has existing territorial disputes with Japan, Taiwan, Vietnam, the Philippines, Malaysia, Indonesia and India. It is surrounded by countries that either have, or are fast developing, nuclear weapons: Russia, North Korea, India, Pakistan and Iran. The opacity of China's decision-making and military spending, and the instinct to conceal its intentions that is deep in its strategic culture, makes China's neighbours deeply uncertain of how it will use its power, even as they become increasingly dependent on their ties to its economy.

China is not alone in being surrounded by mistrustful countries. Japan is yet to live down regional memories of its aggression and colonisation between 1895 and 1945. The ongoing controversies over its war shrines and school textbooks' treatment of its wars betray a lingering suspicion that it is unrepentant about having played a more assertive regional role, and could do so again. India also has been in conflict with, or intervened in, most of its neighbours: Pakistan, China, Bangladesh and Sri Lanka. It has territorial disputes with China and Pakistan and casts a long shadow over Nepal. It is flanked to the north-east and north-west by two nuclear-armed rivals. Similarly, Indonesia has been in conflict or territorial dispute with many of its neighbours: the Philippines, Malaysia, Singapore, East Timor, Australia. All of Vietnam's neighbours have been in conflict with Hanoi in living memory; none much relishes a greater role for Vietnam in continental South-East Asia.

The second dynamic is the cultural rivalries that infect almost every country-to-country relationship in the Indo-Pacific region. Nearly every society there has a profoundly hierarchical social structure domestically, which in turn furnishes it with a framework for interpreting and trying to structure relations with other societies. All are haunted by the memory of domination and cultural borrowing, either from the centres of Sinic or Indic civilisation, or from the Western colonisers who arrived in the sixteenth century and departed only 60 years ago, or both. This makes even the hint of subordination anathema to most Asian countries – particularly its larger ones. Here is another reason why Asia won't simply settle into an ordered hierarchy under Chinese leadership, or indeed under the leadership of any of its major powers. It also means that the likelihood of Asia developing into a closed, cohesive regional bloc – that is able to capture the dynamic benefits of its growing economic integration and leverage its collective weight in global forums – is equally unlikely. Even the most egalitarian of institutions establish a clear ranking of leaders and followers in practical terms, a formal expression of hierarchy that would be very hard for the region's smaller countries to swallow – let alone the big ones that weren't in the lead.

The third dynamic is that powerful forces from outside the Indo-Pacific will play decisive roles in the evolving region. The United States is already central to the current power distribution in the region, and is well aware of the challenge that the rise of the giants poses to its role and preferences in the western Pacific and Indian Oceans. Washington's alliances will remain part of the framework of Indo-Pacific relations for decades to come, though they will not play a role as central as they have for the past 60 years. Despite being mainly focused on Europe and Central Asia, Russia is being drawn into the Indo-Pacific by Asian states' growing appetites for its energy resources and minerals, and for its military hardware. Russia's vast eastern provinces are too vulnerable, and the dynamic rivalries in the Indo-Pacific will be too tempting, for Moscow to ignore its Asian frontiers for long.

The fourth dynamic is the growing economic enmeshment of the region's countries with China. East Asia absorbs 58 per cent of China's exports, and supplies nearly half of China's imports. Much of this intra-regional trade is comprised of production chains, where different components of the same product are manufactured in different countries and then exported to China for final assembly. This is a much more intimate relationship of interdependence than a more traditional production-trade-consumption model. It means that all of China's trading partners have a deepening interest in its economic buoyancy, and they all have a major stake in China's trading successes. Any major trade disputes involving China will have knock-on effects throughout the region, just as any decisions China makes on the value of its currency will have region-wide effects. It also means that as they become integrated into regional production chains that terminate in China, an increasing proportion of Asian countries' own economic fortunes are determined in, and by China. This is a formidable source of influence for Beijing, which it has carefully buttressed by signing economic partnership agreements with every country in South-East Asia, as well as driving a preferential trading agreement with the whole region.

But as China's economic tractor-beam exerts a growing pull on the economic make-up and fortunes of its neighbours, many of them grow increasingly ambivalent about the situation. While there is no uniform reaction to China's rise, there are significant countries in Asia that are unsure of how Beijing will choose to manipulate its growing dominance, and are actively trying to avoid full-spectrum dependence on China. In both elite polling and interview-based studies, strategic thinkers in Japan, South Korea, Vietnam and Indonesia are less than convinced that Beijing's will be a completely benign dominance. The reaction has been the marked tightening of relationships between America and its allies in the Pacific, and the formation of new friendships between Washington and former antagonists such as India and Vietnam. Most significantly, the past five years has seen the growth of tendrils of mutual assistance, investment and strategic co-operation among China's neighbours: Japan with India; India with Vietnam; Korea with Indonesia. These relationships fall far short of formal alliances – for fear of provoking Beijing's sense of isolation – but they are nonetheless important statements of shared perspectives and mutual interests. The result is an uncomfortable dynamic for China: as it grows in power and centrality, so the offsetting agreements and understandings grow around it to hedge in China's growing influence.

But this dynamic is not one that just applies to China. The other major powers also face it to varying extents. Several of India's neighbours have developed or are building similar relationships to offset New Delhi's growing dominance in South Asia. The partnership between China and Pakistan dates from the 1960s. It has allowed Pakistan to become a nuclear armed state to offset India's conventional military dominance, and it serves as an ongoing source of economic and strategic confidence for Islamabad. China has also made significant gains in its relations with Sri Lanka, Myanmar/ Burma and Nepal. Vietnam confronts a similar logic in continental South-East Asia. Well aware of their traditional vulnerability to Vietnamese ambitions, Cambodia and Laos have willingly embraced relationships of comprehensive economic, diplomatic and strategic dependence on Beijing. Thailand and Myanmar/Burma are more sanguine than most about the increasing centrality of China to their fortunes. Further south, Malaysia's optimistic statements about the potential in its relationship with China may be sponsored in part by its awareness of Indonesia's steady economic growth.

The Asia that is emerging will not conform to a neat logic, either of willing acquiescence in being tributaries of a resurgent Middle Kingdom, or coalescing around a new bipolar stand-off between Beijing and Washington. Asia's future will be one of elaborate and overlaid patterns of alignment and enmity, enmeshment and balancing. The growth in power and economic centrality of the giants will be offset by those close to and enmeshed with them seeking to balance their exposure by building relationships with other countries. It will be a world of complex calculations and strategies. It means that, for however fast and long they grow, none of Asia's giants will open up a lead over all the other powers of anywhere near the scale that the United States had after World War II. India and China may grow very big, but so will the countries around them. Asia's power terrain will be very crowded.

The giants, well aware of their vulnerabilities and the jealousies of others, will be paranoid about being isolated and tied down.

This means that if military, financial and gravitational might form the skeleton of the Indo-Pacific order, it is countries' capabilities to establish and block coalitions and partnerships that will form the muscles, the moving parts, of the region. The dynamics of gigantism and rivalry are putting a greater premium on offsetting coalitions and understandings among the giants' neighbours. The deepening of these offsetting alignments only increases the worry of the giants about being surrounded and isolated, and leads them to redouble their efforts in building linkages that block or undercut that possibility. More and more countries in the Indo-Pacific will face a common dilemma: having a national economy that is increasingly tied into China's, but a set of diplomatic and security commitments that are oriented away from China.

These diverging national interests, and the sheer fluidity of the power dynamics of the Indo-Pacific, mean that the formal regional organisations will become less and less relevant. Their meetings will become increasingly stage-managed and formulaic, while the real business of alignment, rivalry, adjustment and confrontation will take place elsewhere. The current pattern of regionalism places ASEAN at the centre because none of the major powers trusts any of the others with leadership, but South-East Asian countries, increasingly drawn apart by the region's power dynamics, cannot hope to play a meaningful role in mediating relations among the giants. The new regional order will be plurilateral, a complex tapestry of overlapping agreements among its countries and with big external players. Countries' economic and security interests will pull in different directions, making clear sets of alignments and confrontation impossible. The sinews of the Indo-Pacific will be both formal agreements and informal understandings, managed flexibly and always under construction or modification as countries calibrate and recalibrate their advantages and disadvantages in the evolving regional dynamic.

Poor little rich country

These are big changes and they will substantially alter the world in which Australia has to make its way. At a very basic level, Australia will become progressively less significant over time. On current growth rates, by the end of this decade China's economy will be nearly ten times as large as Australia's; India's will be two-and-a-quarter times as large; Japan's four-and-a-third times as large; and Indonesia's three-quarters as large. Projected military spending will see Australia's defence budget at just over one-tenth of China's, one-third of India's and one-half of Japan's by 2020. It is more than likely that all of the attributes Australia used to compensate for its small population and economy – technological strength, sophisticated and significant armed forces, alliance with the United States, educated population, and relatively large economy – will decline in importance relative to the countries of Asia during the coming century. Even if the Asian giants' resource hunger doesn't peak until the later 2020s, as some of the optimistic current estimates suggest, new sources of supply currently under development will see Australia's resource production become less important to the region in the medium term, and drop dramatically in importance within a couple of decades. As Europe and North America become less dominant in global economic and strategic terms, as their massive educational and technological leads are closed, Australia's mystique as a Western country within Asia will erode. It may well be that being a rich society in a region dominated by poor great powers may not be a particularly comfortable reputation to shoulder. Ultimately, Australia faces a much harder international situation, in a region dominated by hierarchically minded great powers, where size, dynamism and centrality are used to judge countries' importance.

As time lurches forward to Australia's north, the costs of ignoring the world will mount. Australia's openness to international currents, influences and shocks will remain, but the old techniques of stabilising and making predictable the world around it will gradually lose their bite. In a region shaped by powerful countries with very different preoccupations and preferences, combining great wealth and nagging poverty, growing influence and gnawing paranoia, the flow and cadence of tensions and influences will be arrhythmic and insistent. Relying on happy coincidence may work once in a generation, but when nasty surprises and sudden worrying tensions happen all the time it will call for constant vigilance and careful management. Australia's old 'set and forget' methods of handling international affairs will no longer suffice.

The longest-standing formula in Australia's policy toolkit is the alliance with the United States. All Australian governments since 1951 have rightly regarded it as the cornerstone of Australia's foreign and defence policies. A cast-iron alliance guarantee from the superpower that dominates the oceans through which Australian trade steams, that prints the currency that's used to pay for its exports and imports, that underwrites all the global and regional organisations it negotiates in, that owns space and innovates relentlessly to shape the evolving world, is the gift that keeps giving. Through dumb luck based on common cultural and historical origins, the superpower pays Australia more attention than its size and location would otherwise justify.

Canberra has built on that luck by cleaving as close to Washington as it can for decades. The alliance gives Australia a military and diplomatic heft it could not afford otherwise. It gives it information that makes the world much more predictable than it would otherwise be. America's alliances have aligned Australia's preferences and fortunes so perfectly that it has been lulled into a sense that things should and will always been this way. For the fifty years after 1958, Australia was confident that its alliance complemented America's alliances with Japan, South Korea, Thailand and the

165

Philippines, and that this great wagon-wheel of security guarantees was the anchor that stabilised a potentially dangerous region. Australia agreed with America and its Asian allies and the countries of South-East Asia that hadn't become communist that the stability the alliances provided could be deepened through development, trade and prosperity. And Australia could contribute substantially to that development and prosperity at considerable benefit to itself. Australian minerals, energy and food exports fed Japanese, Korean, Taiwanese and other Asian tigers' reconstruction and development while at the same time providing the money to build a modern, educated, stable and comfortable society at home. Australia's security deal paved the way to its prosperity, and the trade that built its prosperity invested further in the security framework it was part of.

But during the transmillennial decades the alignment started to come apart. Australia's minerals, energy and food began to feed the development of an Asian giant hostile to America's stabilising role in Asia. By 2009 Australia's largest trading partner was America's most serious antagonist. And it wasn't alone: China was also the major trading partner of America's other Asian allies. Australians haven't realised how complicated this situation can be, because Beijing hasn't chosen to contest America's role in Asia too vigorously just yet. China itself is in the awkward situation where the stability provided by the American alliance system is the essential quality that has allowed it to concentrate on its own development and to access the resources and markets that have underpinned its remarkable growth. But every time China's economy doubles in size, every time its new weapons systems come on line, every time its territorial claims rub uncomfortably against those of America's allies, the benefits of stability lose value and the temptation to begin to push back at America's Asian presence increases. As long as American troops are in Japan and Korea, as long as American carrier groups prowl at will along the Pacific's western shore, a host of small countries remain emboldened to block China from asserting its rights. As China grows, America's discomfort deepens. Beijing has made it very conscious of its vulnerabilities – the isolation of the troops and bases it maintains in Japan and South Korea, the long distances its fighters and bombers have to travel from Guam to Asia, the loneliness of its once invincible aircraft carrier battle groups in the vast expanses of the Pacific Ocean. And beneath it all, America knows how much of its yawning debt is financed by China, and how vulnerable it would be should Beijing choose to use its uber-creditor status as leverage.

Washington has started to make adjustments. It has renovated its alliances with Japan, South Korea and Australia. But these are no longer enough. It has deepened its strategic links to countries such as Singapore, which offer its battle fleets vital harbours in the region. America has reached out to former adversaries such as India, Vietnam, and Indonesia, brushing aside high principles and historical grievances that once determined its policies towards those countries. And it has done so because India, Vietnam and Indonesia, along with Japan and South Korea, offer both the heft and the disposition to check and complicate China's schemes for a more authoritative role in the Indo-Pacific. Washington has not signed alliances with New Delhi, Hanoi and Jakarta, because there would be too much opposition on both sides of each prospective alliance. But it doesn't have to. In the new, plurilateral, fluid world that is emerging in the Indo-Pacific, a formal alliance agreement means much less than actual substantive collaboration and common perspectives on the emerging power dynamic. America has every reason to help India, Vietnam and Indonesia grow stronger because the more powerful and confident they are, the more they can constrain and complicate Beijing's designs. In the language of Washington's recent Quadrennial Defense Review and Nuclear Posture Review, India, Vietnam, Taiwan and Singapore are designated 'friends' and spoken of in the same breath as the 'allies' America has had since the 1950s. By small degrees, the nature of America's presence in the Indo-Pacific is shifting. It can no longer rely on its uncontested military supremacy and its alliances as pegs in the sand of the Western Pacific to deal itself into the Indo-Pacific power dynamic. It increasingly has to forge and use new strategic partnerships to help hedge in the Chinese power that with each passing month further exposes America's vulnerabilities in the region.

Strategic choices that determine stability and conflict, that can cost lives and treasure, are made with cold, calculating pragmatism. With these stakes, there can be no room for emotion or sentiment. The brutal truth for Australians is that while Americans will continue to like them as a people, their country and its alliance agreement will become less important to Washington as it faces a rising China determined to push it back towards its own side of the Pacific. Australia may be loyal and comprehensible, but it's not big enough to play a substantive role in complicating China's strategies in the region. The United States will begin to pay much greater attention to the evolving, fluid and complicated relationship among the bigger countries in Asia, because those relationships will determine how involved and influential America can be in the region. It means that Australia will get less of America's attention, and will not be able to count on its support if Washington's strategic interests dictate otherwise. Australia will still gain a great deal from its alliance, and will be well served by continuing to invest in its relationship with Washington. But it should not expect America to be in its corner by default. The alliance will move from being a cornerstone of Australia's international policies to being a major supporting beam – and it will need to be buttressed by other policy beams that will have to be built.

The other default policy in Australia's diplomatic toolkit is multilateralism – meaning a marked preference for dealing with issues through agencies or negotiations involving many countries. Multilateralism is the great equaliser of world politics because it gives smaller countries the chance to put their point across and line up other countries behind their initiatives. Australian leaders and officials realised this early and were part of the creation of the major institutions that shape our world: the United Nations, the International Monetary Fund, the World Bank and the World Trade Organization. They also realised the great value of institutions in their own region, whether or not Australia was a member. ASEAN turned a fractious region into a zone of stability and development. APEC has fostered open trade across the Asia Pacific. In return, multilateralism has been very good to Australia. It worked through the UN to end conflicts in Cambodia and East Timor. It developed the Australia Group and the Nuclear Suppliers Group to make the global uranium trade less amenable to being used by more countries to build nuclear bombs. It formed the Cairns Group to rally agricultural exporters against American and European farming subsidies. In fact, so useful did international institutions become to Australia that multilateralism became the default solution to every troubling issue that arose. Worried about instability and poor economic progress in the Pacific? What about a Pacific Islands Forum? How about unresolved tensions in the Asia Pacific? Try an ASEAN Regional Forum. Flows of asylum seekers assisted by people smugglers? Try a Bali Regional Process on People Smuggling. Competing great powers in Asia? Why not try an Asia Pacific Community? Multilateralism became the band-aid of Australian diplomacy.

The problem is that formal institutions are no longer effective for dealing with a rapidly evolving regional situation. International organisations tend to preserve their memberships, power hierarchies, agendas and decision procedures in stone. They are very hard to change. They can admit new members as required, but find it impossible to exclude members that are no longer relevant.

Those countries that used to be powerful but are no longer stubbornly refuse to countenance a demotion. The result is that regional and global institutions become obsolete as the world around them changes. They continue to meet and issue statements but each year they look more and more like a suburban book club. As the Asia Pacific is superseded by the Indo-Pacific, the Asia Pacific's institutions are relied upon to do less and less heavy diplomatic lifting. The ASEAN Regional Forum and APEC have not had a serious regional agenda to pursue for nearly a decade – because they contain too many countries with no real interest in or influence on Indo-Pacific issues, and exclude too many significant countries with important interests at stake in the emerging regional dynamics.

The result of the basic logic of multilateralism, which makes it impossible to keep institutions relevant to fast changing contexts and difficult to abandon them when they are no longer useful, means that regional and global organisations have multiplied whenever an issue or power constellation changes. After fifty years of this, the international stage has become so crowded with international meetings that one of the hardest jobs of a diplomat is finding dates on which all those who need to are able to attend. As time lurches forward in the Indo-Pacific, change will be constant. Multilateral forums will become more and more irrelevant, and proposing and forming new ones will just not be practical. Attention will shift to negotiating, adjusting, confronting and controlling diverse dynamics using the more flexible sinews of plurilateral relations that are emerging across the Indo-Pacific. This will be deeply challenging for Australia, which has grown comfortable in multilateral contexts and is used to driving its agendas over the course of the year's calendar of regional and global meetings.

Australia felix

As time lurches forward to their north, all of the nostrums that have kept Australians optimistically uninterested in the world beyond their shores are being challenged. Australia is no longer too far away to be affected by the great rivalries and compacts of the world. The Indo-Pacific power highway makes its big sweep from southwards to westwards uncomfortably close to Australia's northern coasts. The new arena of contest and co-operation will be the island chain that spurts out from the Asian landmass to constitute archipelagic South-East Asia. Here is a region of smaller- to medium-sized countries (other than Indonesia) that are heavily trade-dependent, ethnically diverse and still relatively suspicious of each other. All are increasingly drawn in to the economic centre of gravity that is China's economy, and may well soon feel the pull of another centre farther west in India. Together they sit astride the shipping lanes through which close to 70 per cent of the world's seaborne trade passes. This is a fertile region for rivalry, where the Asian giants and the United States will compete to try to build their own and forestall each others' sphere of influence. Australia has never considered itself a South-East Asian country – but it will become one in the eyes of the giants over the next decades. For the first time in history, Australia will be uncomfortably close to the designs and demarches of competing great powers.

This means that in the years ahead, Australia will no longer be too small to make a difference. Its strategic location, as the southern anchor of the island chain dividing the Indian and Pacific Oceans, its geographic size, its resource, energy and agricultural capacities, and its talismanic status as a long-time Western ally of the United States will make Australia into a much richer diplomatic prize in the years ahead. For Beijing to woo Canberra further from its embrace of the United States alliance would be a strategic coup of considerable symbolic weight. But if Canberra quietly integrates with the diplomatic tendrils seeking to forestall the dominance of any of the giants it will mean a great deal to Washington and the other medium- and smaller-sized countries in the region. In other words, Australia will have to get used to the attention and jealousies that come with becoming seen as a bell-wether state. Canberra's choices will not be important enough to tip the region in one or another giants' direction, but they will be important in framing how other medium- and smaller-sized countries interpret the run of power.

As it finds it can no longer rely on the 'set and forget' instruments of the American alliance and multilateral diplomacy to see it through, Australia will need to take the world seriously, study it closely, and choose its actions very carefully. Its first epiphany must be to realise how many countries there are that are in the same situation: American allies or friends, long content to be loyal and concentrate on becoming richer, that have suddenly found their biggest economic partner is China, but are deeply uncomfortable with the full-spectrum dominance of the region by Beijing. The second epiphany is that all of them are closer to China, and that Australia is the only one among them that has never experienced a powerful China. Perhaps Australia has much to learn and much to gain from sharing insights and perspectives on China and increasingly India. The trouble is that Australia has never taken these other countries – South Korea, Vietnam, Thailand, Indonesia, Singapore, Malaysia, the Philippines – as seriously as it will need to now. In the decades ahead, their choices about China, India and America will become as crucial to Australia's security and prosperity as Australia's choices are to them. No country in the region can set and forget. All must continually calibrate the evolving power dynamics in the region and recalibrate their own diplomatic alignments in ways that best serve their own interests.

Canberra must also realise the need to rebalance its centres of attention and effort. For sixty years, Australian policy-makers and diplomats have thought hardest about how to wield influence in two places: Washington and international organisations. Resources have been marshalled, careful analyses compiled, and diplomats have fanned out across the arms of international institutions and arenas of the American government to try to craft decisions Australia's way. All other relationships have been handled pragmatically and properly, but with little thought and less ambition. This will need to change. Canberra will need to maintain and build its influence in Washington – but also in Beijing, New Delhi, Jakarta, Hanoi, Seoul and Tokyo. All these capitals are less open to influence than Washington, but all must be shaped in ways that protect and promote Australia's interests in maintaining the independence, access and safety of the Indo-Pacific's smaller countries. In short, Australia must start to make its own luck – because if it relies on pure serendipity, the twenty-first century will be a very unhappy period in its history.

Time's lurch forward during the transmillennial decades challenges Australia on a greater and more sustained scale than any other period for two hundred years. To remain optimistic and disengaged is to invite decline and humiliation, like so much road kill besides power's highways. This is not a challenge that can be left to the diplomats, even if we choose to resource them at levels appropriate to a nation that has realised that a world less understanding and congenial than it has ever known has suddenly arrived on its doorstep. As Australian society has globalised during the transmillennial decades, so have its international interests and objectives progressively slipped beyond the capacity of a foreign ministry to aggregate and promote. No longer can Australians leave international affairs to the diplomats – because left to their own devices, the diplomats may make the wrong choices. The transmillennial decades have truly dealt Australians an exciting hand: a rising Asia that challenges a nation of insular internationalists to come to terms with their place in the world. It is only by taking responsibility for their fate in a completely new world that Australians will finally realise how lucky they are.

Notes

Introduction

The four scenarios for Asia's future (pages 5–6) are the 'great powers', from Aaron Friedberg, 'Ripe for rivalry: Prospects for peace in a multipolar Asia', *International Security*, 18(3), Winter 1993-94, pp 5–33; the 'concert of Asia', in Coral Bell, *The End of the Vasco da Gama Era*, Lowy Institute Paper 21, Sydney: Lowy Institute for International Policy, 2007; the reversion to tribute/forbearance, in David C Kang, *China Rising: Peace, Power and Order in East Asia*, New York: Columbia University Press, 2007; and 'Chimerica', from Niall Ferguson, 'What "Chimerica" hath wrought', *The American Interest*, Jan-Feb 2009.

1 Australia rising

The description of Australia Day 1990 (pages 11–12) comes from various stories in *The Australian*, Jan 1990; and the economic figures from Ian Macfarlane, *The*

Search for Stability: The Boyer Lectures 2006, Sydney: ABC Books, 2006. The Newspoll results (page 12) were reported in *The Australian*, 25 Jan 1990.

Employment and economic figures c 1990 (page 13) come from ABS data, various years; and the pessimism over Australia's longer-term performance (pages 13–14) is summarised in Peter Sheehan, *Crisis in Abundance*, Melbourne: Penguin Books, 1980.

The impacts on the Australian economy through the 1990s (pages 14–15) are ennumerated in Ken Henry, 'Australia's international engagement and reform', address to the March 2005 Economic and Social Outlook Conference, Melbourne.

The 'catastrophe never came' data (page 16) come from various IMF statistics, <www.imf.org/external/pubs/ft/weo/2010/02/weodata/index.aspx>; the 'miracle economy' quote (page 16) is from Paul Krugman, 'I know what the hedges did last summer', *Fortune*, Dec 1998.

The appraisal of Australian productivity (page 16) is from Graeme Davis and Robert Ewing, 'Why has Australia done better than New Zealand? Good luck or good management?', Treasury working paper 2005-01, Jan 2005; and the benefits reaped (pages 16–17) from John Edwards, *Quiet Boom: How the Long Economic Upswing is Changing Australia and its Role in the World*, Lowy Institute Paper 14, Sydney: Lowy Institute for International Policy, 2006.

The figures comparing Australia's 1990s economy internationally (page 17) come from various IMF statistics; its longer-term performance (page 17) from Dean Parham, 'A more productive Australian economy', *Agenda*, 7(1), 2000; and its historic levels of trade and investment (pages 17–18) from David Parker, 'The importance of open world markets for Australia's development and prosperity', address to the Lowy Institute Conference on Enhancing Transparency in the Multilateral Trading System, Sydney, 4 July 2007.

Population statistics (page 18) come from ABS, 'Population growth: Past, present and future', Australian Social Trends, report 4102.0, June 2010.

Of the three horses in Australia's transmillennial trifecta, global growth (page 19) is described in Ken Henry, 'Australia's economic development', Address to the Committee for the Economic Development of Australia 40th Anniversary AGM Dinner, Sydney, 19 Nov 2001; the emergence of Asia (pages 19–20) in Bryn Battersby and Robert Ewing, 'International trade performance: The gravity of Australia's remoteness', Treasury working paper 2005-03, June 2005; and China's commodity hunger (page 20) in Martin Parkinson, 'Asian economic growth prospects and the impact on Australia', address to the Leading Australia's Future in Asia Program, ANU, Canberra, 18 May 2006.

The resulting effects on Australia's terms of trade (page 21) are described in Ken Henry, 'Revisiting the policy requirements of the terms-of-trade boom', address to the Australian Business Economists, Sydney, 20 May 2008; and Adam McKissack, Jennifer Chang, Robert Ewing and Jyoti Rahman, 'Structural effects of a sustained rise in the terms of trade', Treasury working paper 2008-01, July 2008.

Australia's record at avoiding global downturns (pages 21–22) is presented by John Edwards, 'Australia's experience in the sub-prime crisis', address to the Flinders University International Expert Symposium 'The Subprime Mortgage Meltdown: Origins, Trajectories and Regional Implications', Adelaide, 16 May 2008; and the relatively small impact of drought (page 22) in Lan Lu and David Hedley, 'The impact of the 2002–2003 drought on the economy and agricultural employment', *Treasury Economic Roundup*, Autumn 2004.

The summary of Australia's post-1990 terms of trade (pages 22–23) is from David Gruen, 'A tale of two terms-of-trade booms', address to the Australian Industry Group Economy 2006 Forum, Melbourne, 1 March 2006.

The figures of Australia's boom economy (pages 24–25) come from Edwards, *Quiet Boom*, p 54.

Hugh White's assessment of defence spending (page 26) is in his *Beyond the Defence of Australia: Finding a New Balance in Australian Strategic Policy*, Lowy Institute Paper 16, Sydney: Lowy Institute for International Policy, 2006.

Hu Jintao is quoted (page 27) from 'Building a better future together for a China-Australia partnership of all-round co-operation', speech to the Federal Parliament of the Commonwealth of Australia, 24 Oct 2003; and Alexander Downer's announcement (page 28) from his media conference, Beijing, 17 Aug 2004.

On the transmillennial enrichment of average Australians (page 29) see Commonwealth Treasury, Australian Net Private Wealth reports, various years; and ABS, 'Household income and income distribution', report 6523.0, Australia, 2007-08; while on this wealth's distribution (page 30) see Xavier Sala-i-Martin and Sanket Mohapatra, 'Poverty, inequality and the distribution of income in the Group of 20', Treasury Economic Roundup Autumn 2003; and Ann Harding, Mandy Yap and Rachel Lloyd, 'Trends in spatial income inequality 1996 to 2001', AMP-NATSEM Income and Wealth Report, no 8, Sept 2004.

On iPods as wealth indicators (page 30) see Craig James, 'Commsec iPod Index: Something for nothing', *Commsec Economic Insights*, 4 Oct 2007; and the same for luxury car sales (page 31) see his 'The Commsec luxury car index', *Commsec Economic Insights*, 21 March 2007; 'Luxury car sales near record highs', *Commsec*

Economic Insights, 14 July 2010; and 'SUV sales surge to record highs', *Commsec Economic Insights*, 16 Aug 2010.

Population and housing figures (pages 31–32) come from James Bond, 'Recent developments in the Australian housing market', Treasury Economic Roundup Summer 2003-04; and Edwards, *Quiet Boom*, p 56.

The Lowy Institute's surveys (page 32) are recorded in Fergus Hanson, *Australia and the World: Public Opinion and Foreign Policy*, The Lowy Institute Poll 2008, 2009 and 2010, Sydney: Lowy Institute, 2008–2010; the figures on household debt (pages 32–33) from Michael Davies, 'Household debt in Australia', BIS papers no 46, Bank of International Settlements, <www.bis.org/publ/bppdf/bispap46e.pdf>; Karen Maley, 'Our dangerous debt affair', *Business Spectator*, 20 Sept 2010; and David Uren, 'Household debt rises as mortgages grow', *The Australian*, 20 April 2010.

Marriage statistics (page 33) are analysed in ABS, 'Family formation: Age at first marriage', Australian Social Trends report 4102.0, 19 June 1997; education figures (page 33) in Gene Tunny, 'Educational attainment in Australia', *Treasury Economic Roundup*, Autumn 2006, <www.treasury.gov.au/documents/1107/PDF/01Educational.pdf>; family planning (page 33) in ABS, 'Population growth: Past, present and future', Australian Social Trends, report 4102.0, June 2010; and ABS, 'Family formation: Trends in childlessness', Australian Social Trends, report 4102.0, June 2002; and the 'sea change' phenomenon (pages 33–34) in ABS, 'Population distribution', Australian Social Trends, report 4102.0, 23 July 2008.

2 The great convergence

On the selection of Huawei (page 36) see Doug Young, 'Huawei shows China's scope for organic growth', *Reuters*, 21 Jan 2010; and for the company's background (pages 36–37), Winter Nie, 'How Chinese companies test global waters: The Huawei success story', *Dow Jones*, 10 Sept 2010.

On Ren Zhengfei's adoption of Maoist strategies (page 37) see Jane Macartney, 'Mao's tactics mean business' *The Times* (London), 9 Aug 2005.

On telephony transmission standards (pages 37–38) see Philip Qu and Carl Polley, 'The new standard bearer', *IEEE Spectrum*, Dec 2005; and the Chinese government's support of Huawei (page 38) Craig Simons and William Underhill, 'The Huawei way', *Newsweek*, 16 Jan 2006.

Huawei's policies on innovation and employee incentive (page 38) are covered by Sunny Li Sun, 'Internationalisation strategy of MNEs from emerging economies: The case of Huawei', *Multinational Business Review*, 17(2), Feb 2009; and its strategy for international expansion (page 39) by Jennifer Chen, 'Dragon aloft', *Ottawa Citizen*, 9 June 2005.

On Huawei's branding (page 39) see Andrew Murray-Watson, 'Huawei? Who are they?', *The Independent*, 9 Sept 2007; and its placement in international telephony league tables (page 40) Jason Dean, 'Huawei: Shunned in the US, growing fast everywhere else', *Wall Street Journal*, 22 Feb 2008.

The analysis of the global economic divide (page 42) comes from Gregory Clark, *A Farewell to Alms: A Brief Economic History of the World*, Princeton: Princeton University Press, 2008; and that of the gulf between population and production (page 42) from Angus Maddison, *The World Economy: A Millennial Perspective*, Paris, OECD, 2001; and Kenneth Pomeranz, *The Great Divergence: China, Europe, and the Making of the Modern World Economy*, Princeton: Princeton University Press, 2001.

Stephen Krasner is quoted (page 43) from his *Structural Conflict: The Third World against Global Liberalism*, Berkeley: University of California Press, 1985, p 4.

For China's immediate post-Mao priorities (page 45) see Ross Garnaut, 'Twenty years of economic reform and structural change in the Chinese economy' in Ross Garnaut and Ligang Song (eds), *China: Twenty Years of Reform*, Canberra: Asia Pacific Press, 1999; and its later relaxation of restraints (page 46) see Jane Golley and Ligang Song, 'Chinese economic reform and development: Achievements, emerging challenges and unfinished tasks', in Ross Garnaut, Jane Golley and Ligang Song (eds), *China: The Next Twenty Years of Reform and Development*, Canberra: ANU EPress, 2010.

The ensuing dilemmas, such as bus-driver strikes (page 46), are covered in Harry Harding, *China's Second Revolution: Reform after Mao*, Sydney: Allen & Unwin, 1987.

The 2010 figures on China's economy, average wealth, production and trade (page 47) come from the IMF database, <www.imf.org/external/pubs/ft/weo/2010/02/weodata/index.aspx>; and those of average income, number of billionaires and trade league table (page 47) from Wayne M Morrison, 'China's economic conditions', CRS Report for Congress, Washington DC: Congressional Research Service, 11 Dec 2009.

For Vietnam's 1986 land reforms (page 48) see Khong Vu, 'Economic reform and growth performance: China and Vietnam in comparison', East Asia Institute Seminar, National University of Singapore, 18 Sept 2008; and its economic reforms up to 1990 (page 48) David Dollar, 'Reform, growth and poverty in Vietnam', Policy Research Working Paper, The World Bank, May 2002.

The 2008 economic data for Vietnam (pages 48–49) comes from the IMF database, <www.imf.org/external/pubs/ft/weo/2010/02/weodata/index.aspx>.

India's 'abject position' in 1991 (pages 49–50) is described in Mark Thirlwell, *India: The Next Economic Giant*, Lowy Institute Paper 1, Sydney: Lowy Institute for International Policy, 2005; and its problems with 'patronage and incumbency' (page 50) in Francine R Frankel, *India's Political Economy 1947–2004: The Gradual Revolution*, New Delhi: Oxford University Press, 2005.

For India's economic policies through the 1990s (pages 50–51) see Kalpana Kochhar, Utsav Kumar, Raghuram Rajan, Arvind Subramanian and Ioannis Tokatlidis, 'India's pattern of development: What happened, what follows', Working Paper 06/22, Washington DC: IMF, 2006; and for the data on the results (page 51), the IMF database, <www.imf.org/external/pubs/ft/weo/2010/02/weodata/index.aspx>.

The assessment of *The Economist* (page 51) comes from 'India's surprising economic miracle', 2–10 Oct 2010.

On the entanglement of the state and military with Indonesia's economy (page 52) see Wing Thye Woo, Bruce Glassburner and Anwar Nasution, *Macroeconomic Crisis and Longterm Growth: The Case of Indonesia 1965–1990*, Washington DC: World Bank, 1994; and for its post-Suharto reforms (page 53) Yuri Sato, 'Post-crisis reform in Indonesia: Policy for intervening in ownership in historical perspective', IDE research paper no 4, Tokyo: Institute for Developing Economies, Sept 2003. The ensuing policies of decentralisation (page 53) are described in Sherry Tao Kong, 'Economic and political transition in China and Indonesia', <www.eastasiaforum.org>, 4 Aug 2010.

The economic data of Indonesia's recovery (page 53) come from World Bank, 'Indonesia economic quarterly: Looking forward', Washington DC: World Bank, Sept 2010.

The analysis of the growth and social management of the 'tigers' (page 54) is described in Frank B Tipton, *The Rise of Asia: Economics, Society and Politics in Contemporary Asia*, Melbourne: Macmillan, 1998; the inability of the 'giants' to do the same (pages 54–55) in L Alan Winters and Shahid Yusuf (eds), *Dancing with Giants: China, India and the Global Economy*, Washington DC: World Bank, 2007.

Mark Thirlwell's term the 'great convergence' (page 55) is in his 'The great convergence', International Economy Comments no 4, Sydney: Lowy Institute for International Policy, 9 Nov 2010.

The data on Asian poverty c 1980 (pages 56–57) comes from the World Bank database, <data.worldbank.org/data-catalog>.

The figures for the impact of corruption in India (page 59) are from Edward Friedman and Bruce Gilley (eds), *Asia's Giants: Comparing China and India*, New York: Plagrave Macmillan, 2005.

The figures for mobile phone use in the Asian giants (page 60), come from World Bank, *World Development Indicators 2009*, Washington DC: World Bank, 2009.

On Asian diasporas (pages 61–62) see AnnaLee Saxenian, *Silicon Valley's New Immigrant Entrepreneurs*, San Francisco: Public Policy Institute of California, 1999.

3 The geometry of power

The 'two Chinese professors' (page 67) are Hu Angang and Men Honghua, 'The rise of modern China', quoted in David M Lampton, *The Three Faces of Chinese Power: Might, Money and Minds*, Berkeley: University of California Press, 2008.

The issue of the number of great powers (page 68) is raised in Kenneth and Waltz, *Theory of International Politics*, New York: McGraw-Hill, 1979.

Daryl Copeland's idea of 'a heteropolar world' (page 69) is in his *Guerrilla Diplomacy: Rethinking International Relations*, Boulder: Lynne Rienner, 2009.

On Taiwan–China friction (page 70) see Greg Austin (ed), *Missile Diplomacy and Taiwan's Future: Innovations in Politics and Military Power*, Canberra Papers on Strategy and Defence no 122, Canberra: ANU Strategic and Defence Studies Centre, 1997; and on general South-East Asian alarm at China's militarism (pages 71–72) see Suisheng Zhao, *Power Competition in East Asia*, Basingstoke: Macmillan, 1997.

On the formation of modern states (page 72) see Charles Tilly, *The Formation of National States in Western Europe*, Princeton: Princeton University Press, 1975; on the failings of Soviet 'command power' (page 73), see David Lake, 'Beyond anarchy: The importance of security institutions', *International Security*, 26(1), Summer 2001.

The Monroe doctrine (pages 73–74) is described in Brian Loveman, *No Higher Law: American Foreign Policy and the Western Hemisphere since 1776*, Chapel Hill: University of North Carolina Press, 2010.

Regarding countries' tendency towards protectionism during downturns (page 75) it is interesting to note that after the global financial crisis, the largest economic slump since the recession, there has been no large-scale retreat into protectionism among the world's major economies, as there was during the Great Depression.

China's and India's 'gravitational' effects (pages 76–77) are dicussed in Mark Thirlwell, *Second Thoughts on Globalisation: Can the Developed World Cope with the Rise of China and India?* Lowy Institute Paper 18, Sydney: Lowy Institute for International Policy, 1997.

The statistics on the growth of multilateralism (pages 80–81) come from the Union of International Associations database, <www.uia.be/stats>.

The joining of Asia (page 87) is described in Anthony Bubalo and Malcolm Cook, 'Horizontal Asia', *The American Interest*, May-June 2010; and the trade figures (pages 86–87) come from the UNCTAD Handbook of Statistics, <www.unctad. org/Templates/Page.asp?intItemID=1890&lang=1>.

4 The psychology of power

For Hindu/Malay hierarchicalism (page 96) see Anthony Read, *South-East Asia in the Age of Commerce 1450–1680*, New Haven: Yale University Press, 1988; and the Confucian version (pages 96–97) in Arthur Waley, *Three Ways of Thought in Ancient China*, Stanford: Stanford University Press, 1982. Maintaining rank distinction (page 97) is described in Louis Dumont, *Homo Hierarchicus: The Caste System and its Implications*, Chicago: University of Chicago Press, 1970.

On 'civilisation' (page 98) see Norbert Elias, *The Civilizing Process*, trans Edmund Jephcott, Malden: Blackwell, 1994; for Asian cultural assertions thereof (page 98) see John K Fairbank, 'China's foreign policy in historical perspective' in *China Perceived: Images and Policies in Chinese-American Relations*, New York: Alfred A Knopf, 1974. On the Chinese emporer (page 98), see John Fairbank (ed), *The Chinese World Order: Traditional China's Foreign Relations*, Cambridge(Mass): Harvard University Press, 1968; and for outcasts (page 98),

Norimitsu Onishi, 'Japan's outcasts still wait for acceptance', *New York Times*, 15 Jan 2009.

Otto von Gierke's quote (page 99) comes from his *Political Theories of the Middle Age*, trans FW Maitland, Cambridge: Cambridge University Press, 1927, pp 20–21; Michael Howard's (page 100) from his *The Invention of Peace: Reflections on War and International Order*, New Haven: Yale University Press, 2000, p 24.

On colonial-era Western rudeness (page 101), see Kenneth Pyle, *Japan Rising: The Resurgence of Japanese Power and Purpose*, New York: Century Foundation, 2007, ch 4; and its control of Asian staples (page 101), in John Fairbank and Edwin Reischauer, *China: Tradition and Transformation*, Boston: George Allen and Unwin, 1979, pp 307–46.

Asian colour preferences (page 102) are discussed in Barry Sautman, 'Anti-black racism in post-Mao China', *The China Quarterly*, 138, 1994; the European hierarchy of races (page 102) is likewise in Ivan Hannaford, *Race: The History of an Idea in the West*, Baltimore: Johns Hopkins University Press, 1996.

Industrial Japan's 'self-loathing' (page 103) is covered in Eika Tai, 'Rethinking culture, national culture, and Japanese culture', *Japanese Language and Literature*, 31(1), 2003; and in Chung Yong-Hwa, 'The modern transformation of Korean identity: Enlightenment and orientalism', *The Korea Journal*, Spring 2006; and China's 'mortification' (page 103) in SCM Paine, *The Sino-Japanese War of 1894–1895*, Cambridge: Cambridge University Press, 2003.

For Western scholars' views of Asia (page 103) see Benedict Anderson, *Imagined Communities: Reflections on the Origin and Spread of Nationalism*, London: Verso, 1991, pp 163–64.

The 'mozaics of ethnicities' (page 104) comes from Grant Evans (ed), *Asia's Cultural Mosaic: An Anthropological Introduction*, New York: Prentice-Hall, 1993; and 'prickly nationalism' (page 105) from Stein Tonnesson and Hans Antlov, 'Asia in theories of nationalism and national identity', in Tonnesson and Antlov (eds), *Asian Forms of the Nation*, Richmond: Curzon, 1996, p 22.

On Asian countries fitting in to international arenas (page 106), see Hedley Bull and Adam Watson (eds), *The Expansion of International Society*, Oxford: Clarendon Press, 1984.

The 'inner liberation' (page 107) is described in Partha Chatterjee, *The Nation and its Fragments*, Princeton: Princeton University Press, 1993, p 26; and Nehru's spiritualism (page 108) in JN Dixit, *India's Foreign Policy 1947–2003*, New Delhi: Picus Books, 2003, pp 14–15.

For the 'deeply unjust' global order (page 109) see Stephen D Krasner, *Structural Conflict: The Third World against Global Liberalism*, Berkeley: University of California Press, 1985; and for the Cancun meeting (pages 111–112) see Robert Baldwin, 'Failure of the WTO Ministerial Conference at Cancun: Reasons and remedies', *The World Economy*, 29(6), May 2006.

The BRICS acronym (page 113) is from Dominic Wilson and Roopa Purushothaman, 'Dreaming with BRICS: The path to 2050', Goldman Sachs Global Economics Paper no 99, Oct 2003.

On Chinese concern at US maritime power (page 116) see Michael Wesley (ed), *Energy Security in Asia*, London: Routledge, 2007; while on its own 'responsibility' (page 117) see Yong Deng, *China's Struggle for Status: The Realignment of International Relations*, Cambridge: Cambridge University Press, pp 270–76.

For the predictions re China having the largest economy by 2020 (page 117) see Goldman Sachs Global Economics Group, *BRICS and Beyond*, Goldman Sachs, 2007; and for Lowy Institute polling (pages 117–118), see Fergus Hanson and Andrew Shearer, *China and the World: Public Opinion and Foreign Policy*, Sydney: Lowy Institute for International Policy, Oct 2009.

Arthur Schopenhauer is quoted (page 118) from his 'The wisdom of life' in *Essays From Parerga and Paralipomena*, trans T Barley Saunders, London: Allen & Unwin, 1951, p 92; John Fitzgerald (page 118) from his 'Introduction: The dignity of nations', in Sechin YS Chien and John Fitzgerald (eds), *The Dignity of Nations: Equality, Competition and Honour in East Asian Nationalism*, Hong Kong: Hong Kong University Press, 2006, p 3.

Skin whitening (page 119) is discussed in Eric PH Li, Hyun Jeong Min, Russell W Belk, Junko Kimura, and Shalini Bahl, 'Skin lightening and beauty in four Asian cultures', *Advances in Consumer Research*, 35, 2008.

On Asian sensitivity to slights (page 120) see James Bowman, *Honor: A History*, New York: Encounter, 2006, p 27; and on supporting sports teams (page 120) see Daniel Bell, *China's New Confucianism: Politics and Everyday Life in a Changing Society*, Princeton: Princeton University Press, 2008, pp 91–97.

5 Insular nation

The 'Free Schapelle' stickers (page 122) were reported in 'Bumper protest calls for boycott', *Gold Coast Bulletin*, 31 May 2005; the 'pulse of outrage' (page 122) in Peter Charlton, 'White powder diplomacy' *Courier Mail*, 4 June 2005; 'Threats, anger over Corby trial' and 'Corby anger hits new highs', *West Australian*, 31 May 2005. That Australians' reactions were based on stereotypes (page 123) was noted by Tony Parkinson, 'Now the ugly Australian', *The Age*, 3 June 2005; and poll figures (page 123) quoted from Alan Sipress, 'Drug case renews rancour in Pacific', *Washington Post*, 4 June 2005.

Trade and investment figures (page 124) come from David Parker, 'The importance of open world markets for Australia's development and prosperity', address to the Lowy Institute Conference on Enhancing Transparency in the Multilateral Trading System, Sydney, 4 July 2007; and John Edwards, *Quiet Boom: How the Long Economic Upswing is Changing Australia and its Role in the World*, Lowy Institute Paper 14, Sydney: Lowy Institute for International Policy, 2006, p 54.

Demographic figures (pages 124–25) are drawn from ABS, 'Family formation: Cultural diversity in marriages', Australian Social Trends, report 4102.0, 4 July 2000; those for international travel (page 125) from ABS, 'Holidaying abroad', Australian Social Trends, report 4102.0, Sept 2010.

The long list of expats (page 126) is quoted from Michael Fullilove and Chloe Flutter, *Diaspora: The World Wide Web of Australians*, Lowy Institute Paper 04, Sydney: Lowy Institute for International Policy, 2004, pp 5–6.

Julia Gillard is quoted (page 127) from 'Foreign policy is not my things, says Gillard', ABC News, 6 Oct 2010, <www.abc.net.au/news/stories/2010/10/05/3030339.htm>; Tony Abbott from his 'National security fundamentals', speech to the Lowy Institute for International Policy, Sydney, 23 April 2010. The two researchers interviewing Laurie Brereton (page 127) were Allan Gyngell and Michael Wesley, for their book, *Making Australian Foreign Policy*, Melbourne: Cambridge University Press, 2003. On John Howard's statements re foreign affairs (pages 127–28) see Michael Wesley, *The Howard Paradox: Australian Diplomacy in Asia 1996–2006*, Sydney: ABC Books, 2007.

The figures on Australian diplomatic missions (page 128) are from Lowy Institute, *Australia's Diplomatic Deficit: Reinvesting in our Instruments of International Policy*, Blue Ribbon Panel Report, Sydney: Lowy Institute for International Policy, 2009; the Lowy Institute's research re broadcasting (page 128) is in Annmaree O'Keeffe and Alex Oliver, 'International broadcasting and its contribution to public diplomacy', Lowy Institute Working Paper, Sydney: Lowy Institute for International Policy, 2010.

Asylum-seeker arrivals (page 129) are ennumerated in Janet Phillips and Harriet Spinks, 'Boat arrivals in Australia since 1976', Parliamentary Library Background Note, Canberra: Parliament of Australia, 23 Sept 2010; the cost of Nauru detention centre (page 129) in Kazimierz Bem, Nina Field, Nic Maclellan, Sarah Meyer and Tony Morris, 'A price too high: The cost of Australia's approach to asylum seekers', A Just Australia and Oxfam Australia, Aug 2007, <www.oxfam.org.au/resources/filestore/originals/OAus-PriceTooHighAsylumSeekers-0807.pdf>.

Hedley Bull is quoted (page 130) from his 'Australia and the great powers in Asia', in Gordon Greenwood and Norman Harper (eds), *Australia in World Affairs 1966–1970*, Melbourne: Cheshire, 1974, p 325; Ross Garnaut (page 131) from his *Australia and the Northeast Asian Ascendancy: Report to the Prime Minister and the Minister for Foreign Affairs and Trade*, Canberra: AGPS, 1989, pp 2–3; and Paul Keating (page 131) from his 'Australia, Asia and the new regionalism', 1996 Singapore Lecture, Singapore: Institute of Southeast Asian Studies, Jan 1996, p 7.

Australians' attitudes to foreign countries (page 131) are recorded in Fergus Hanson, *Australia and the World: Public Opinion and Foreign Policy*, The Lowy Institute Poll 2008, 2009 and 2010, Sydney: Lowy Institute, 2008–2010; Asian language statistics (pages 131–32) from John Fitzgerald, Robin Jeffery, Kama Maclean and Tessa Morris-Suzuki, *Maximising Australia's Asia Knowledge: Repositioning and Renewal of a National Asset*, Canberra: Asian Studies Association of Australia, 2002.

Australia's 'major fears' post-WWII (page 132) are discussed in CP Fitzgerald, 'Australia and Asia', in Gordon Greenwood and Norman Harper (eds), *Australia in World Affairs 1950–1955*, Melbourne: FW Cheshire, 1957.

Fears of Asian 'invasion' (page 133) are covered by David Walker, *Anxious Nation: Australia and the Rise of Asia 1850–1939*, Brisbane: University of Queensland Press, 1999; the debate over 'Asian values' (pages 134–35) by Stephanie Lawson, 'Cultural relativism and democracy: Political myths about "Asia" and the "West"', in Richard Robison (ed), *Pathways to Asia: The Politics of Engagement*, Sydney, Allen & Unwin, 1996.

Geoffrey Blainey's memorable phase 'the tyranny of distance' has become embedded in our national psyche (page 136), despite the fact that most of those who have used the phase have never read the book: *The Tyranny of Distance: How Distance Shaped Australia's History*, Melbourne: Sun Books, 1966.

Sir John Crawford is quoted (page 137) from his 'Australia as a Pacific power', in WGK Duncan (ed), *Australia's Foreign Policy*, Sydney: Angus & Robertson, 1938, p 71; Hugh Mackay likewise (pages 137–38) from his and Rebecca Huntley's *The IPSOS Mackay Report: Exploring the Mind & Mood of Australia*, Sydney: IPSOS Australia, 2001 and 2003.

On the Ottawa Agreements (page 139) see Crawford, 'Australia as a Pacific power', p 78.

On Australia and Asian energy security (page 140) see Richard Leaver, 'Australia and Asia-Pacific energy security: The rhymes of history', in Michael Wesley (ed), *Energy Security in Asia*, London: Routledge, 2007, p 92; William Cohen is quoted (page 141) from James Cotton, *East Timor, Australia and Regional Order: Intervention and its Aftermath in South-East Asia*, London: Routledge-Curzon, 2004.

For intelligence-sharing (page 143) see Jeffrey Richelson and Desmond Ball, *The Ties that Bind: Intelligence Cooperation between the UKUSA Countries: The United Kingdom, the United States of America, Canada, Australia, and New Zealand*, Boston: Allen & Unwin, 1985.

On the Howard government's scepticism re international organisations (page 144) see Wesley, *The Howard Paradox*.

For the argument the US alliance compromises Australia (page 145) see Philip Bell and Roger Bell, *Implicated: The United States in Australia*, Melbourne: Oxford University Press, 1993; and Alison Brionowski, *Allied and Addicted*, Melbourne: Scribe, 2007. On US bases as nuclear targets (page 145) see Joseph A Camilleri, *Australian–American Relations: The Web of Dependence*, Melbourne: Macmillan, 1980, pp 124–26; and Australia as terrorist target (page 145), Alison Broinowski, 'Bali as blowback', *The Sydney Papers*, 15(2), Autumn 2003.

For calls to abandon the US alliance and 'embrace and Asian future' (page 145) see Mark Beeson, 'Australia's relationship with the United States: The case for greater independence', *Australian Journal of Political Science*, 38(3), Nov 2003.

For the split of opinion over Australia's true 'region' (page 146) see Fergus Hanson's various reports: *Australia and the World: Public Opinion and Foreign Policy*, The Lowy Institute Poll 2008, 2009 and 2010, Sydney: Lowy Institute, 2008–2010.

6 Here comes the world

Pre-European Asian trade (pages 148–49) is described in Janet Abu-Lughod, *Before European Hegemony: The World System 1250–1350*, Oxford: Oxford University Press, 1991; and Aztec rituals (page 149) in Manuel Aguilar-Moreno, *Handbook to Life in the Ancient Aztec World*, New York: Facts on File, 2006.

On Henry the Navigator (page149–50) see Peter Russell, *Prince Henry 'The Navigator': A Life*, New Haven: Yale University Press, 2000.

For China's imperial period (page 156) see John Fairbank and Edwin Reischauer, *China: Tradition and Transformation*, Boston: George Allen and Unwin, 1979; and its current use of gravitational power (page 156), Yong Deng, *China's Struggle for Status: The Realignment of International Relations*, Cambridge: Cambridge University Press, 2008.

China's naval strategy (page 157) is discussed in Malcolm Cook, Raoul Heinrichs, Rory Medcalf and Andrew Shearer, *Power and Choice: Asian Security Futures*, Sydney: Lowy Institute for International Policy, 2010.

My thanks to Mark Thirlwell for suggesting the scenario concerning Shanghai and Mumbai becoming global financial centres (pages 157–58).

On the nations surrounding China (pages 158–59), see Andrew Nathan and Robert Ross, *The Great Wall and the Empty Fortress: China's Search for Security*, New York: WW Norton, 1997; on Asian rivalries (page 159) see Wang Gungwu, *Bind Us in Time: Nation and Civilization in Asia*, Singapore: Times Academic Press, 2002.

Regarding other Asian nations' fears of China's rise (page 161) see Bates Gill, Michael Green, Kiyoto Tsuji and William Watts, *Strategic Views on Asian Regionalism: Survey Results and Analysis,* Washington DC: CSIS, Feb 2009. In particular they note that, when Washington's Centre for Strategic and International Studies interviewed security elites in nine Asia-Pacific countries in 2002, most responded that China represented the greatest potential threat to the region's stability in the next ten years.

On ASEAN (page 163) see David Jones and Michael Smith, 'Making process, not progress: ASEAN and the evolving East Asian regional order", *International Security*, 32(1), 2007.

The projections of Australia's vs Asian giants' economies (page 164) are based on current IMF data: <www.imf.org/external/pubs/ft/weo/2010/02/weodata/index.aspx>; those on military spending (page 164) on data from the International Institute for Strategic Studies, *The Military Balance,* London: Routledge, 2010; and the future of Australia's mineral boom (page 164) from Ric Battelino, 'Mining booms and the Australian economy', speech to the Sydney Institute, Sydney, 23 Feb 2010.

China's benefits on the US alliance system (page 166) are explained in Avery Goldstein, *Rising to the Challenge: China's Grand Strategy and International*

Security, Stanford: Stanford University Press, 2005; while America's discomfort at China's rise (pages 166–67) in Roger Cliff, Mark Burles, Michael Chase, Derek Eaton and Kevin Pollpeter, *Entering the Dragon's Lair: Chinese Anti-Access Strategies and their Implications for the United States*, Santa Monica: RAND Corporation, 2007.

The US Defense review (pages 167–68) is *Annual Report to Congress: Military Power of the People's Republic of China*, Washington DC: Office of the Secretary of Defense, 2009.

On Australian multilateralism (page 169) see Allan Gyngell and Michael Wesley, *Making Australian Foreign Policy*, 2nd edn, Melbourne: Cambridge University Press, 2007.

Index